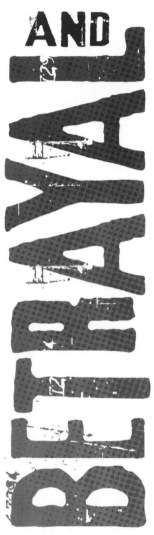

LOVE AND BETRAYAL

LOVE AND BETRAYAL

STORIES OF HOPE TO HELP YOU HEAL FROM YOUR HUSBAND'S PORNOGRAPHY ADDICTION

CARMEL PARKER WHITE, PhD, AND NATALIE BLACK MILNE

CFI
An Imprint of Cedar Fort, Inc.
Springville, Utah

ISBN 13: 978-1-4621-2037-6

Published by CFI, an imprint of Cedar Fort, Inc.
2373 W. 700 S., Springville, UT 84663
Distributed by Cedar Fort, Inc., www.cedarfort.com

LIBRARY OF CONGRESS CATALOGING-IN-PUBLICATION DATA
Names: White, Carmel Parker, author. | Milne, Natalie Black, author.
Title: Love and betrayal: stories of hope to help you heal from your
    husband's pornography addiction / by Carmel Parker White and Natalie Black
    Milne.
Description: Springville, Utah : CFI,An Imprint of Cedar Fort, Inc., [2017] |
    Includes bibliographical references and index.
Identifiers: LCCN 2017003643 (print) | LCCN 2017010565 (ebook) | ISBN
    9781462127948 | ISBN 9781462120376 (pbk. : alk. paper)
Subjects: LCSH: Pornography--Religious aspects--Church of Jesus Christ of
    Latter-day Saints. | Sex addiction--Religious aspects--Church of Jesus
    Christ of Latter-day Saints. | Sex addicts--Rehabilitation. |
    Pornography--Psychological aspects. | Husband and wife.
Classification: LCC BX8643.P64 (ebook) | LCC BX8643.P64 W45 2017 (print) |
    DDC 241/.667--dc23
LC record available at https://lccn.loc.gov/2017003643

Cover design by Shawnda T. Craig
Cover design © 2017 by Cedar Fort, Inc.
Edited and typeset by Rebecca Bird

Printed in the United States of America

10 9 8 7 6 5 4 3 2 1

Printed on acid-free paper

To my mother.
You have always encouraged me
to face life and its challenges head-on.
I am thankful to have your love and example
to help me through life's arduous journey.
—Carmel

To J. P. V.
I will be eternally grateful for the
love and guidance you provided me during
the most difficult time of my life. You have
been my biggest advocate for writing this book.
—Carmel

To women everywhere who suffer the
consequences of a loved one's choices.
—Natalie

CONTENTS

PREFACE

s there anyone who hasn't known at least one family member or friend with a pornography problem? How many people have experienced marital strife or divorce because of pornography? Has there been a recent general conference where pornography has not been mentioned? Pornography is no longer the elephant in the room that no one wants to talk about. However, there is a side to pornography use and addiction that continues to evade the attention it deserves. The LDS discussion of pornography tends to focus on helping the viewer or addict, neglecting to mention how pornography hurts those close to the addict. When a husband repeatedly views pornography or is battling a pornography addiction, his wife will also experience its devastating impact in many ways that are difficult to comprehend or predict when the addiction first comes to light.

We interviewed over a dozen women whose husbands habitually used pornography. This book is a result of those interviews. We felt humbled as women shared their painful stories and the powerful insights they had gained. If pornography has become a part of your marriage, this book can give you a sense of what you will be facing in the future: the issues that emerge when pornography is first discovered, the problems that might occur that impact your well-being, and the concerns that will appear whether or not you stay married.

In our interviews, we talked to some women who had known about the problem for years and others who had recently discovered it. A few women reported that their husband had started using pornography sometime during their marriage, while for other women it had been present their entire marriage. Almost all the women had children of different ages. Their stories are very personal and quite poignant. While there were commonalities, each woman dealt with her husband's addiction in her own way. As these narratives attest, there is no one right way, no road map, to navigate through having pornography in your marriage.

OTHER AUDIENCES

While the primary audience for this book is LDS women who have dealt with their husband's pornography addiction, others may benefit from this book. We've identified four additional groups who could benefit from learning about women's "lived experiences" with pornography in their marriage:

1. Priesthood Leaders. Once a pornography problem has been disclosed, most women we interviewed turned first to their bishop or stake president for guidance and direction in dealing with their husband's addiction. While many of these Church leaders were trained on how to handle addictions, few knew how to support the wives of the addicts. Thus, it is our hope that by reading this book, priesthood leaders might be better able to counsel with wives.

2. Young Adult Women. Unfortunately, the commonness of pornography addiction and related problems means that many of today's young adult women will encounter some kind of pornography addiction in those they date or marry. It is wise that these women have some basic education in these matters before courtship and marriage. Some women we interviewed knew about their husband's pornography use before they were married and still felt that the Lord approved of their marriage. However, they also wished they would have known more about what and how to ask about a pornography addiction and also about what it would mean for their marriage. We hope that this book will allow young adults to look at the problem with their "eyes wide open." Some have even suggested that the best question to ask a young man you are dating is not "Is pornography a problem for you?" but rather more in-depth questions such as: "When was the last time you saw pornography?" or "What has been your

involvement with pornography?" (in order to have an accurate picture of the problem). Some young women are counseled that pornography use will disappear once a man marries and has an acceptable sexual outlet. The women we interviewed and therapists agree that this does not happen.

3. Other Women. Even women who do not have pornography in their marriage will be able to learn about how this problem impacts other women. The chances are very high that a sister, cousin, ward member, or close friend is dealing with this problem. Women who have pornography as part of their marriages are often not open about their situation and instead suffer silently. Having a better understanding of how women feel when their spouse is using pornography can lead other women to be more compassionate and supportive.

4. Husbands and Other Men. Finally, it may help a husband who has a pornography addiction to understand more clearly how women feel about pornography and how his addiction directly impacts his marriage, as well as his wife's emotional, physical, and spiritual well-being. If the wife is experiencing betrayal trauma, she will need to heal before she can actively work on healing the marriage. At times, some women's behaviors and emotions seem out of proportion to the problem, but understanding betrayal trauma can help a husband comprehend why his wife is acting the way she is.

CAUTION

Parts of this book may be difficult to read. It can be painful to read women's stories and to learn of the heartache and suffering they have experienced, especially if there are personal similarities to your situation. While we don't intend to shock or sensationalize, we do share true stories that represent women's daily experiences. Viewing pornography is sexual in nature and influences men's sexual behaviors; therefore, it follows that there will also be open discussions of sexuality in this book. Alice, one of the women we interviewed, felt that because pornography is one of Satan's greatest tools, it needs to honestly be addressed. We subscribe to her approach.

She said,

> I ask myself: Am I in Relief Society, or is it okay to say it how it really is? I have determined that we have to start calling it what it is. It is okay to call it *pornography*. It might be abrasive, but it is what it is. I am definitely past the point of tiptoeing around it. Satan doesn't give it any respect, so it is best to just call it what it is.

FORMAT OF THE BOOK

The chapters in this book generally follow this format: a brief exploration of the topic or principle at the beginning of the chapter. The topics are integrated with women's comments about that topic. After discussing the topic, we have included the story of one of the women we interviewed. Finally, when appropriate, quotes from a marriage and family therapist, Dr. Kevin Skinner, are included. Dr. Skinner has also heavily contributed to our understanding of betrayal trauma.

OUR THANKS

Many individuals have contributed to conducting the research and preparing the manuscript. We appreciate Cynthia Winward, Maria Johnson, Valerie Owens, and Brent Melling who read drafts of this book; Sue Wilkey, Chad Olsen, and Kim Hansen who contributed to the research process and read some of the women's stories; and most of all to the women who let us into a personal part of their mortal experiences.

INTRODUCTION

The mist of darkness will cover you at times so much that you will not be able to see your way even a short distance ahead. You will not be able to see clearly. But you can *feel* your way. With the gift of the Holy Ghost, you can *feel* your way ahead through life. Grasp the iron rod, and do not let go.

– Boyd K. Packer[1]

Discovering that your husband has been using pornography is painful, life altering, and confusingly traumatic for women. Sadly, discovering that a partner is using pornography is only the first step of a long process of healing and recovery. We interviewed over a dozen women in May 2014 and have heard countless stories from other women who have shared how their life has been impacted by their husband's pornography use. We share these women's stories and insights with the hope that their experiences will bring to light the emotional and spiritual needs of women whose husbands have serious pornography problems.

Women we interviewed were all different, and no two women had the same experience in discovering or dealing with their spouses' pornography use. For example, some women had husbands who were motivated to honestly try to recover, whereas others had husbands who were not at all interested or merely pretended they were interested in recovery. While some husbands had affairs or engaged in other types of sexually acting-out behaviors, most of the husbands had problems only with pornography and masturbation. Further, each woman was unique in her personality, her reaction to discovering and dealing with pornography, and her approach to her own recovery and healing. Through the very different stories we share in this book, it becomes obvious that there is not one right way to move forward when pornography is part of a marriage; no "one-size fits all" approach. Each woman we interviewed had to personally decide what to do when pornography use was disclosed or discovered.

In spite of their emotional and spiritual pain, the women we interviewed demonstrated amazing strength in their difficult and uncertain journeys of recovery. Some were empowered to reach out and support other women who were also living with pornography in their marriages. The resilience and strength of the women we interviewed was apparent, even though at times they felt ill equipped and overwhelmed in knowing how to deal with pornography in their marriages. Cynthia[2] told us, "The feeling that comes from just knowing that *you are not alone* in this struggle is powerful." Amber wanted other women to know that they "*do not have to be alone* in this." Alice talked about how much support she felt connecting with other women in her support group. She said,

> A lot of women don't tell anyone because they are so embarrassed or ashamed of their husband's addiction. Because I've connected with other women, I realize that *I am not alone in my struggle* to forgive a man that I love so much and other times that I hate so much. *I am not alone* in the heartache and the betrayal. This support group has been the biggest blessing for me because the women there have reassured me that I am not crazy for the feelings that I have; that *I am not the only one* experiencing this.

Women often suffer alone because of the shame associated with their husband's pornography use, especially as they interact with other members of the Church who view pornography as a serious sexual sin. The feelings of isolation and loneliness, along with not being able to talk openly about something that permeates every aspect of their life, causes women to feel angry, frustrated, and lonely.

PREVALENCE OF PORNOGRAPHY

Pornography has become an epidemic in society, and the Church is no exception. Sixty-four percent of men in the United States view pornography at least monthly, and Christian men's viewing habits virtually mirror this.[3] While it is not easy to find data on LDS men, Hart and Weaver have said that "Latter-day Saints are no different when it comes to the prevalence and magnitude of sexual addictions."[4] The number rises significantly to 77 percent for men ages eighteen to thirty. Another unsettling statistic is that in 56 percent of divorces in the United States, one partner has an obsessive interest in pornographic websites.[5] Pornography use increases the marital infidelity rate by more than 300 percent.[6]

Elder Quentin L. Cook has referred to pornography as a plague,[7] and others call it the modern-day plague afflicting the elders of Israel. However, many users fail to realize that pornography doesn't just hurt them. John Hilton III and Anthony Sweat have said, "Pornography hurts everyone involved with it. . . . Pornography does not just affect the participant, but it also affects those around him. It leads to immorality, destroys marriages, and contributes to sex crimes, all of which have a negative effect on society. Pornography is not an 'isolated' sin; it's a social one."[8]

Elder Jeffrey R. Holland declared, "[Pornography] ought to be seen like a public health crisis; like a war; like an infectious, fatal epidemic; like a moral plague on the body politic that is maiming the lives of our citizens."[9] Because pornography use and accessibility has become so widespread, measures taken to fight it become important. For instance, on March 11, 2016, the Utah Legislature passed a resolution declaring pornography a public health crisis—the first state in the United States to do so.[10] Such measures are taken in hopes of raising awareness of the pandemic pornography use has become.

Pornography use can range in frequency, duration, and type. After an initial exposure to pornography, viewing can become repeated, habitual, and for some, a full-blown addiction. Elder Dallin H. Oaks identifies four levels of involvement with pornography: inadvertent exposure (accidental exposure to pornography), occasional use (intentional use designed to stir sexual feelings and behaviors), intensive use (pornography viewing that has become a habit), and compulsive use (when an addiction or a dependency on pornography is developed).[11] The difference between intensive or compulsive use seems quite slight, and men's observable behavior will likely be similar for either intensive or compulsive use. Further, intensive use can easily slip into compulsive use. If men are trying to minimize their pornography use, it may be that they tell themselves and others that it is not an addiction but rather just a bad habit. A qualified mental health professional, someone who specializes in sex addictions, is the most appropriate person to determine if a person's pornography use is habitual or if it is an addiction. Whether it is a habit or an addiction, the neurological pathways that are created when using pornography are the same and have the same devastating effects on a relationship. William M. Struthers discussed the neurology pathways that are developed when using pornography:

> These associations are seared into the fabric of the brain. These memories can then be pulled up at any time and replayed as private sexual fantasies. In sexual fantasy, the neurological circuit is replayed, further strengthening it. The result is an increase in autonomic sexual arousal, which requires an outlet. These memories and fantasies keep him in bondage and worsen the consequences of the earlier behavior. It can prevent him from being truly present in a marriage, being more preoccupied with the images than focused on his wife.[12]

ADDICTION AND BEHAVIOR

When a husband's pornography use has become habitual or compulsive, which was the case for the women we interviewed, wives encounter the difficulties of living with someone who has an addiction. Cynthia told us, "I have spent the last seven months coming to know what it means to live with someone who is addicted to something." To be clear, not everyone who views pornography is addicted to pornography, just as not everyone who drinks alcohol is an alcoholic. Using Elder Oak's classification, some may use pornography occasionally but not habitually or compulsively. According to the American Society of Addiction Medicine (ASAM), "Addiction is a primary, chronic disease of brain reward, motivation, memory and related circuitry. Dysfunction in these circuits leads to characteristic biological, psychological, social and spiritual manifestations. This is reflected in an individual pathologically pursuing reward and/or relief by substance use and other behaviors."[13]

Similar to other chronic diseases, addiction often involves cycles of relapse and remission. ASAM further indicates that addiction is characterized by an "inability to *consistently* abstain," "impairment in behavioral control," "craving[s]," "diminished recognition of significant problems with one's behaviors and interpersonal relationships," and "dysfunctional emotional response[s]."[14]

A pornography addiction is considered one type of sexual addiction. The Sexual Recovery Institute, founded by Robert Weiss, defines sexual addiction as a "persistent and escalating pattern or patterns of sexual behaviors acted out despite increasingly negative consequences to self and others."[15] Spouses are the ones who most likely experience those negative consequences because of the intimate nature of the marital relationship. Some of the out-of-control repetitive acts of sex addicts include the following: masturbation, pornography, simultaneous or repeated sequential affairs, cybersex, phone sex, multiple anonymous partners, unsafe sexual activity, partner sexualization, objectification, strip clubs, adult bookstores, and prostitution.

NEGATIVE CONSEQUENCES OF PORNOGRAPHY ADDICTION

There may be several negative consequences for someone who has a pornography addiction. Table 1 (see page 6) describes some possible negative consequences of sexual addiction in the social, emotional, cognitive, financial/occupational, and spiritual areas. These negative consequences may directly or indirectly influence women and the marital relationship.

Living with an addict is lonely and can cause one to feel isolated. When a husband is preoccupied in his own thoughts about the images he has viewed, he can become emotionally distant. This emotional unavailability is one of the reasons that many women told us they were lonely in their marriage. As a newlywed, Ashley frequently wondered why her husband was not interested in connecting with her.

> When he would come home, he would always just go lie down and look at his phone. He never wanted to be with me. I was that pathetic wife who had cleaned the house and wanted to have dinner together, and he was always too tired or had a headache or wasn't feeling well. I would go into the room and try to cuddle up to him, and he wouldn't want to. I would try to kiss him, and he would just turn away. Every day I would make sure the house was cleaner than the day before, that the meal I prepared was better than the day before, and that I was more attractive than the day before, but with him it seemed that nothing was ever good enough.

TABLE 1. POSSIBLE NEGATIVE OUTCOMES FOR SEXUAL ADDICTS[16]

Domain	Negative Outcomes
Emotional	Increased stress from family life and work High anxiety Increased shame and guilt due to a lifestyle that is often inconsistent with personal values, beliefs, and spirituality Higher levels of depression Easily bored Constant fear of discovery Compartmentalized and suppressed emotions, inability to maintain an integrated, holistic view of self
Cognitive	Strong desire for novel experiences Increased distractibility Difficulty maintaining attention and focus
Financial/ Occupational	Increased debt for purchase of pornography or other types of sexual activities Decrease in work productivity Job loss Expensive inpatient or outpatient therapy
Spiritual	Loss of the Spirit Unworthy to participate in priesthood blessings and ordinances Loss of temple recommend Church discipline

For some women, this emotional absence over time made them feel like they were not really married or that they were merely living with a roommate rather than a husband.

Another problem that comes with emotional unavailability is that the husband is no longer an equal and engaged partner who is able to deal with life's challenges together with his wife, including issues that arise in the family. Many addicts want to avoid pain and stress and may use pornography to deal with the stress. During those times of high stress when the husband needs to be fully engaged, he could be coping with stress by using pornography, making him even more emotionally unavailable to his wife. Sarah, whose story is shared in chapter 1, told us how their move to

Georgia to start graduate school was incredibly stressful for her, but Hank did not seem as stressed by the situation. Later she learned that Hank was using pornography to cope with the stress.

Viewing pornography literally makes long-lasting (sometimes permanent) physiological changes. The delicate cluster of nerves that processes all our visual stimuli and indeed the very brain that regulates our bodies' normal sexual functioning, learns new pathways and develops different patterns of neurochemical responses through the viewing of pornography. Repeated viewing strengthens these aberrant patterns to such a degree that scientists using crude brain imaging technology can literally see the effects of pornography on the brain.[17] Several women told us that they thought pornography had altered their husband's brains. Claire, who was frustrated with her husband's preoccupied thinking, asked us, "Why can't he focus? Why can't he get through a sentence? I think his brain is damaged. He will continue to be this way until we can put a stop to the addiction." Claire's husband would also unknowingly drive through red stoplights. Other women reported that when their husbands were using pornography, they would become more forgetful or couldn't remember things.

A few women worried about what their husband's pornography use meant for his occupation and their finances. Especially if he was viewing pornography at work, the fear of him losing his job and losing the family's income added more fear and uncertainty. Furthermore, the cost of treating a pornography addiction can be prohibitive for many couples, especially if they are young. Sarah told us how they took out additional student loans to pay for Hank's therapy with a sex therapist. Other couples who opted for inpatient treatment of the addiction reported that it could cost upwards of $30,000. Couples who felt inpatient treatment was the best option for them would have to reach out to family, friends, and the Church to assist them in financing the treatment. Melanie describes the many funding sources they used in trying to pay for Doug's inpatient therapy.

> We did the longest treatment offered at the inpatient facility and it was $27,000.00. My family decided they could give us $4,000. His parents were able to come up with some money to go toward his stay at the inpatient treatment center. It was still not nearly enough money, so we talked to our bishop and our stake president. They were will-

ing to try and help us, but they also said that we needed to foot the bill as much as we could, which was understandable because we were not in a very big ward. I really didn't want to take money from other people's fast offerings. So we spent some time discussing this problem and finally decided that we just needed to tell people. We needed to let others know what was going on and that we needed help. So we decided to make a Facebook page and we invited a bunch of people to join us in accomplishing what we were trying to do, and it was scary [but successful]. I think the Church only had to pay $6,000 out of the $27,000.

A couple of women whose husbands had been in counseling or in an expensive inpatient treatment program expressed frustration that while they had spent thousands of dollars on treatment, their husband's pornography use had not stopped. For example, Claire said, "We have spent anywhere between $25,000 to $30,000 on counseling and other programs. What I finally realized is that until he is willing to do what these programs recommend he does or what the counselor says, we are just wasting our money. So we have stopped spending money on counseling and on programs." Spending this amount of money for an inpatient treatment that hasn't resulted in behavioral changes may feel like another type of betrayal.

As you will see in the following chapters, the negative consequences of a pornography addiction can cause incredible strain in a marriage and cause women a great deal of pain and for some, a form of trauma referred to as betrayal trauma. As you read these stories and principles that are illustrated in the stories, we hope that you will find insight, guidance, and peace that can only be given by relying on the Savior and His love.

BETRAYAL TRAUMA 1

But Jesus said unto him, Judas, betrayest thou the Son of man with a kiss?

— Luke 22:48

Recent research shows that pornography damages the wife of the pornography user in significant ways.[18] Most women experience *betrayal trauma*, a very real and severe emotional response. "Betrayal trauma refers to the damage that is caused when someone experiences a betrayal in their primary relationship that damages the trust, safety and security of the bond they have with their partner."[19] Alice contrasts the trauma of living with pornography in her marriage to the trauma she experienced at an event earlier in her life:

> I was in the Reno race arena a few years ago when that airplane crashed and killed twelve people there. We had box seating there and there were fatalities on both sides of our box. Twelve people died, and ninety people lost limbs. I saw people die. I saw people bleeding, and it was so bad. I really saw horrific things. I sat right next to a lady in a brown dress who didn't make it. My dad kept telling me that if I didn't get into therapy, he was going to fly down and take me himself, but what he didn't realize was that on a trauma scale, my marriage had been far more traumatic than this event. I've been able to get past this event. It was hard, and it still makes me nervous to think about it. I go back every year with a group of people for a memorial, and it is always really emotional, but it still pales in comparison to what I have

experienced in my marriage. I received so much attention, love, and support through this that I have been able to move past it because it was a one-time plane crash, it was a one-time event. But how do you forgive someone who crashes a plane into your marriage every day? Over and over again?

Alice concludes, "The big deal is really not about the porn, or the strip clubs, or the prostitutes, or the affairs. It is about the lies. I have been more hurt by the dishonesty than anything else." When a husband lies about his pornography use, the trust, safety, and security of the marital bond is severely damaged.

When a husband's pornography habit comes to light, it is not uncommon for his spouse to experience trauma from this form of betrayal. Psychological trauma has not always been well understood or appreciated, but it can have profound and devastating effects. Betrayal trauma can occur when one person betrays, abandons, or refuses to provide support to another in a close, personal relationship such as marriage. In other words, the person we trust becomes our source of pain.[20]

In betrayal trauma, our significant other has violated explicit or implicit trust.[21] The relationship that once brought safety and security now brings fear and uncertainty. The assumption that your spouse can be trusted is completely erased. Therapists and researchers now recognize the psychological damage that occurs when people feel betrayed or victimized by someone who they are close to, someone who typically supports and loves them. Betrayal trauma represents the loss of a *real* actual thing—the marriage and relationship women thought they had.

Someone suffering from betrayal trauma can experience symptoms similar to post-traumatic stress disorder such as anxiety, depression, frequent mood-swings, excessive emotions, obsessiveness, hypervigilance, disconnectedness, and compulsive behaviors.[22]

> Either sudden or protracted discoveries of sexual and/or romantic betrayal by a long-term partner represents a profound and recurring psychological trauma for those who endure it, similar to those suddenly losing a job, child, or home, and . . . the subsequent behaviors of those experiencing or learning of this relational betrayal . . . are consistent with trauma response.[23]

Betrayal trauma is often overlooked or misunderstood by others around us. This trauma can cause strong emotional reactions, intense psychological pain, and an inability to cope. Because this emotional trauma increases the levels of stress hormones, there can also be physical impacts on your body, which also adds to the difficulty of dealing with the trauma. Living with pornography in a marriage can cause a wife to feel violated and unsafe in her closest and most intimate relationship.

In order to fully understand betrayal trauma, we need to understand attachment theory. Beginning in infancy, we develop attachments based on interpersonal relationships with others. Attachment theory states that when a child is hurt, becomes alarmed, or perceives a threat, he or she seeks to be in close proximity to his or her attachment figure, typically his or her mother. The child finds emotional, psychological, and physical comfort and security from that relationship, like a safe-haven for the child. When the child is in a threatening situation and is separated from his or her mother, he or she often acts distressed or anxious.

As the child matures, he or she continues to seek relationships that provide emotional, psychological, and physical comfort when there is a threat or when she experiences some type of pain, fear, or uncertainty. Later, as one develops romantic relationships and eventually marries, the comfort and security now comes from the romantic partner or the spouse, rather than the parent. Spouses are expected to be the source of support for each other and to provide emotional and psychological comfort during difficult times. Discovering a pornography addiction or another type of sexual addiction turns positive attachment feelings into feelings of insecurity and danger. Steffens and Means describe this as a fundamental shift in the relationship:

> All the warmth, safety, joy and comfort that the relationship formerly held can no longer be counted on. The relationship now becomes a source of danger, because you've discovered that much of what you believed about the one you love was a lie.[24]

Betrayal trauma is also called an attachment injury. Steffens and Means illustrate how quickly the relationship between a husband and wife can change.

> In one moment of life, security is replaced with betrayal. . . . The partner knows that the person with whom he or she lives, sleeps and invests time and feelings in participates in hidden sexual behaviors that jeopardize his or her finances, safety, health and even her life, not to mention their children. Prior to this discovery, the person believed his

or her partner loved only him or her and remained faithful. Suddenly, their relationship holds danger and dark secrets. Discovering that much of your life is built on lies proves traumatizing and destroys one's sense of safety and security."[25]

You read earlier in this chapter how Alice's husband's pornography use and the accompanying lies caused a great deal of trauma for her. Other women we interviewed told us similar things. Melanie said, "I catch myself obsessively worrying sometimes, and I cannot do that. I was sick often with stomachaches, headaches, and just random things. I was stressing out over what he was doing." Claire said, "I have told him multiple times that I wished he just smoked so that I could see and smell when he was using. Then I could stop looking for that bad feeling to hit me and the light to go out of his eyes." Liz said,

> Upon initial discovery, I felt like since I had no control over what he was doing that I needed better control of my house and my kids. I tried to keep the house spotless, make better meals, and have the kids more in control. I felt like if I were a better wife, housekeeper, or cook, then he would want me more. It was a really manic thing for me, because some days I was so depressed I could do nothing, but other days I wanted everything perfect and to have control over everything.

The way a husband and wife bond is an intricate puzzle. Researchers are only starting to understand what happens to the chemistry of our brains and bodies when we form an intimate relationship. What researchers do know is that the connection between a husband and wife causes them to operate in sync with each other. Each partner regulates the blood pressure, heart rate, breathing, and hormone levels of the other. Therefore, when this attachment is breached or damaged, our physical, mental, emotional, and spiritual health can be altered in painful and powerful ways. Now instead of grounding us, this form of betrayal puts us in free fall. This betrayal overwhelms our coping capacities and defines the relationship as a source of danger rather than a safe haven.[26]

We interviewed Dr. Kevin Skinner, an LDS therapist who specializes in working with women who have experienced pornography in their marriage and the resulting betrayal trauma. Throughout the book, we include portions of our interview. He explained the concept of betrayal trauma as follows:

I use a PTSD model when defining and treating betrayal trauma. Some symptoms of betrayal trauma include reliving the experience; having a lot of fear, fear of the unknown, indescribable fear; avoiding people, places, and locations that are associated with the trauma (e.g., going to a mall, going to a public swimming pool, watching certain television shows, and sometimes any television shows); increased emotional arousal which comes from anger and irritability, which may be emotions that they haven't experienced a lot of in the past. There is also a cognitive part of the betrayal trauma, where women think, *There is something wrong with me. I'm not good enough.* All of these symptoms are associated with some type of betrayal within the relationship. It can be pornography or it can be sexually acting out in other ways.

With secrecy and lying in the relationship, the first question the brain is designed to ask is, "Am I safe in this relationship?" Then the next questions asked are "Am I lovable? Am I desirable? Am I a person of value?" In a marriage, one of the things that we believe is that this person we are with is going to protect us and that we are going to be safe with them, not just physically, but emotionally. When pornography or other sexual betrayal enters in then they begin to impede on that natural feeling of safety and we now wonder, "Am I safe with this person?" "Do I know this person? They have lied to me; they've deceived me; they have talked one way but acted another way. So, do I really know them?" Biologically we are not wired to connect with people with whom we do not feel safe, which is a pretty normal response to fear or trepidation.

According to Dr. Skinner, one of the sources of women's fear is that they start to ask, "If you're willing to lie about this, what else are you willing to lie about?" He shared some research that has been done on infidelity by Peggy Vaughn and how open communication about the details help couples stay together.

Vaughn found that couples who stay together were the ones who were more willing to talk about the details. I believe that what we take from that research is that if a husband who has been viewing pornography is not willing to talk about the details, then the natural inclination of the wife is to feel like there are things that he is not telling her, which means there is more. So, the details can be very helpful in settling the mind down. "I can wrap my mind around what this is, but if you don't have more to tell me then my mind doesn't have parameters and it will make it worse because I really don't know."

Generally speaking, pornography is a method of sexually acting out, and the wife can wonder about other ways her husband is acting out but not telling her. Most people today, in this LDS culture, are not acting out in other ways and my data shows that. Pornography and masturbation are the most frequent. In fact, when you compare LDS population to other religious groups, members are less likely to be having affairs or going to topless bars.

Women shared with us the betrayal they felt discovering their husband's pornography use, but that many felt that the lies were the worst part. Robert Weiss, a therapist, said that betrayed spouses have every reason to feel incredible pain. It is not just anyone who caused this pain, loss, and hurt; a betrayed spouse's feelings are magnified by the fact that they've been cheated on and lied to by the one person they most depend upon for their own security.

Think what it would be like to have your best friend—the person you live, sleep, and have sex with, the one who co-parents your children and with whom you share your most intimate self, your finances, your world—suddenly becomes someone coldly unknown to you. The person who carries with them the most profound emotional and concrete significance in your past, present, and future has just taken a sharp implement and ripped apart your emotional world (and often that of your family) with lies, manipulation, and a seeming lack of concern about your emotional and physical wellbeing![27]

We conclude this chapter with Sarah's story. Her story illustrates how painful it was to learn about her husband's pornography use. In fact, she referred to the experience as her own "Liberty Jail" trial. In Liberty Jail, Joseph Smith pleaded with the Lord to help him understand why he and the other Saints were suffering and why at times He seemed so distant. This feeling of being alone, suffering, and feeling the Lord is distant is common among the women we interviewed. Sarah had been married to Hank for a little over three and a half years when we interviewed her, and it was obvious that she had a deep love for him. In fact, her love for Hank seemed even more painful when she learned about the pornography and his lying about his use of it.

SARAH'S STORY

I met Hank in college. What I really liked about him was that he seemed really confident in his own skin and he was never manipulative or controlling. He had just returned from a mission, had a strong testimony, was active in the Church, and attended the temple. He was a breath of fresh air, and we instantly clicked. After a very short time, I told myself that I was going to marry this guy. We just fit—we were perfect for each other. We started dating in November and were engaged in March. It felt fast for me, but I also felt that this was what God wanted me to do.

A week after our engagement, Hank and I had been kissing and he put his hands somewhere they didn't belong. We both felt horrible about it. We felt like we needed to talk to the bishop. Sunday morning came, and Hank pulled me aside and said, "There is something else I need to talk to you about." He went on to tell me that in the past he had struggled with pornography and masturbation. I remember being completely shocked. I asked him, "How far in the past?" He said, "Last Tuesday." That seems funny now, but at the time I was completely unprepared for his disclosure. I thought to myself, *That's a really short past.* One of the first things Hank said after telling me was, "Oh, I feel so much better now." I thought, *Are you kidding me? This is not supposed to be happening to me.* I knew I wasn't perfect but I was kind of a naïve, goody-goody girl, and I was completely shocked by his confession. Growing up, I had dressed modestly, participated in Young Women, and had good friends. Hadn't I done the right things to guarantee having a husband who didn't look at pornography? He asked me what I was thinking. Two things came out of my mouth: "The Atonement is real. I feel really fat right now."

We went to church and I was still in shock mode. It was all kind of a blur. I became more confused when we met with the bishop. When Hank had confessed to me his problem, he was very remorseful and even cried. He felt horrible. But sitting there in front of the bishop, he showed no remorse and was very matter-of-fact when he talked about it. During our talk with the bishop, the main issue became what he and I had done. Looking back, it is obvious now that telling the bishop about his pornography use had become routine for him. He had told the bishop, "I look at pornography when I am alone and bored." Later on when I met with the bishop individually, he told me, "Just so you know, I would never have let you marry him if he had not told you about the pornography. I really think that from what Hank has told me, he's not an addict." The bishop kind of diagnosed him for me. So I was quite relieved. Hank was not addicted to pornography. Then the bishop said that he thought that once Hank could express his sexuality in marriage, the pornography problem would go away.

From that point on I felt like our engagement was very traumatic. We had already announced it to everyone and had set a date, but I didn't know if I should move back the wedding date to be sure about where things were with Hank's pornography use. I went to my dad for advice. My dad told me that this is a common battle that all men face. He reminded me that when it comes to male sexuality, men are very visual. He then read Doctrine and Covenants 121:37, which talks about covering our sins and exercising control or dominion over others. My dad said, "Look, he has never tried to control you like all your other boyfriends have. He is not covering his sins; instead he is bringing them to light. If you still want to marry him, he has opened up this great channel of communication for the rest of your marriage." My dad did not tell me if I should marry Hank or not. But he did point out that Hank was doing a lot of things right. I *knew* that God wanted me to marry Hank. My patriarchal blessing tells me to listen to my priesthood leaders, and my bishop told me that Hank was not an addict. At this point, Hank's pornography was limited to magazines, mostly magazines at the grocery store and at big-box bookstores. So I felt good about getting married and we went forward with it.

During our engagement, Hank traveled a lot. He was gone most weekends. He told me that this is when he would struggle the most with the temptation to view pornography. It was hard on him to be alone, and his work was stressful. I told him that he could call me anytime he felt tempted, and we would work through it together. This seemed to help him. When he was not away for work he would call me early every morning and we would go work out together. This also seemed to serve as a necessary distraction, because for some reason mornings were another time he was tempted to view pornography. We were totally "white knuckling"[28] it to the temple. Our engagement was really a stressful time, but I kept telling myself that if we could get through the engagement and get married, then I could fix him with all the sex he needed and the problem would just go away.

I told Hank that even though he was not an addict, we should probably try the addiction recovery meeting through the Church. He agreed and we both went to one meeting. We felt uncomfortable. We really thought that we were okay because Hank was not an addict and everyone else there was. When I went to the women's 12-step group, I pitied them. I was so judgmental of them. I was embarrassed I was even there. I was not going to become one of them. I would make sure this never happened in our marriage. I vowed to myself that I was going to give him enough sex and fix him. Even when we had kids, I'd still give him sex all the time so it would never come down to what we witnessed with these couples. We both hated going to the 12-step meeting. We never went again.

Looking back now, I would have done so many things differently during our engagement. The first thing you need to know is that an addict is really good at minimizing the problem and lying about it. You need to ask for specific numbers about everything and realize that when an addict says "three," it is a lot more than that. I would want to see a written down timeline that included the first time he was exposed to pornography, the first time he masturbated, the first time he sought pornography out on his own, and how long he would look at it. I would also want to know how long he would engage in that cycle of viewing and masturbating before he stopped and went to talk to his bishop, how many different bishops he had seen, and how soon he would relapse after talking to his bishop. Then with all that information, I would go see a certified sex therapist to help talk me through this information before getting married. I really was clueless about addiction in general, but more specifically pornography addiction. I later asked him when his "bad habit" turned into an addiction. He told me, "Honestly, I was powerless over it the first time I masturbated. I was addicted from that point on."

Well, we made it to the temple to get married. He loved me, and he was always paying attention to me sexually and in other ways too. He wanted sex all the time. This was really overwhelming at first. I committed myself to have sex with him at least once every day (except around the time I had our son) to help him with his temptations. I gave him sex whenever he wanted it, because this was going to help him stop looking at pornography. I told myself that it really doesn't take that long, that he is a good man, and if this is how he wants me to show love to him, then I will be the good wife and do it. I have learned recently that the frequency of our sex did not help him stop looking at pornography. Instead, at times, our daily sex actually allowed him to complete fantasies that he had started earlier in the day when he viewed pornography.

Hank was never a jerk or mean to me. In our marriage he would overcompensate in so many other areas, such as saying his prayers, reading his scriptures, and attending the temple. I put him on this pedestal because he was so much better than I was in doing those things. He initiated family home evening and all the other spiritual things in our family. I have since asked him if that was to mask the addiction. He told me that it wasn't. It was more of him trying so hard to do everything he was supposed to do so the addiction would go away. I could truly see him trying to do all the things that different bishops over the years had counseled him to do. He was trying to perform his way out of his addiction. Even though I thought we had a great marriage, I still had no clue that he was still involved with pornography.

During this time, he would also say little things that led me to believe that the pornography was really gone. He would make minimal confessions to me. For example, after returning from a college trip that I didn't go with him on, he said, "I can't believe they dropped us off at the mall on a Sunday just to kill time. I didn't want to shop, so I went to the bookstore. Those magazines were so tempting." The way he said it made me believe that he had just glimpsed at them, but in reality, he had opened them up and spent a lot of time looking at scantily-clad women. But I totally trusted him. I always thought he was being honest with me. When he would tell me those types of things I would think to myself, *Oh, he is so good at communicating with me. He is telling me when he is struggling.* The reality was that they were fake confessions, and he was minimizing his involvement with pornography as well.

Another thing that bothered me about those first few years was his choice of gifts for me. He would always want to give me lingerie for my birthday. He would be looking at it and say, "That is exactly what I want. You should ask for that for your birthday." That really was the last thing I wanted. Just before he finally confessed everything, I should have clued in to what was going on when he bought me a Brazilian bikini wax for Mother's Day. Of course that is how every mother wants to celebrate motherhood—ripping the hair out of your skin until it hurts!

The Internet was not a problem for him during the first two years of our marriage. He stuck with books and magazines. When we moved out of state for graduate school, that all changed. Our move was super stressful. Everything that could have possibly gone wrong did. We had to move three different times before settling into an apartment because our first one was full of fleas and the second one had bedbugs. It was horrible, absolutely horrible. I had a panic attack—I mean a full-blown panic attack. I couldn't breathe. I don't have any history of mental illness, but I had a hyperventilating panic attack. I was the crazy one. I couldn't believe how well he was managing the stress. I now realize that porn medicates his anxiety pretty well. He was constantly medicating while I was a mess. It's a good thing I didn't find out about his Internet porn then. That would have been disastrous. When we hooked up the Internet in our apartment, he insisted that I put blockers on the computer. I told him, "I'm putting these up but I know you can get around them."

He said, "I know. I just want it to prevent pop-ups." So, unknown to me, when he wanted to look at porn, he would just type in the password, unblock it, and then re-download it after he was finished. I held on to the false security of, "Oh, that's so nice that he's doing that to prevent pop-ups from tempting him. He is dealing with this temptation so well." Unfortunately, however, that summer before graduate school is when his addiction really took off. He said the longest he was able to go without viewing pornography once he was in graduate school was six weeks. I felt guilty anytime I left Hank alone. He would always tell me how hard it was for him when I wasn't there. He was under the impression as much as I was that I helped him stay sober. I am naturally a very independent person, but I put aside my independence so that I could help him.

During his first year of graduate school, I thought the month of December was a great month for us. His brother was getting married and Hank had time off from school and could do his other work online, so we flew home to spend the entire month with his family. We visited the temple three times while we were there: twice for weddings and once for a session. Sexually, everything was really good that month and we continued to have sex every day. We were inseparable for that entire month. After New Year's Day, Hank had to fly back to go to school. Meanwhile, my parents flew my son and me down to visit them. The morning before Hank flew back to school and I left to visit my parents, I made sure we had sex in hopes that it would be enough to help him get through temptations the week without me being there. We were apart for one week.

Hank picked me up from the airport. When we were driving home I told him that I had missed him. I started touching him, and he wasn't responsive at all. I asked, "Did you look at pornography? Did you slip up?"

He said, "Yeah, I did." I was instantly in shock and I turned away from him.

I asked "When?" He said, "When I first arrived back home. It was that night."

I asked "How long?" He replied that it was about five minutes. I asked, "So you pulled down the blocker to look?" and he answered "Yeah." I was shocked and kind of numb. I didn't know how to react. I was totally quiet but my body was definitely reacting. After he dropped me off at home, he had to go back to school. That is when I finally let myself cry. When he got home later that evening, I don't remember the details, but I had sex with him because I wanted to make sure he still wanted me, and I wanted to help him not to be tempted by pornography anymore. That is one of the times I look back on and I feel the most empathy for myself. It is so sad that I was in that much pain and still had sex with him. I was still trying to fix him with the only resource I had—my body.

After having sex Hank fell asleep. I couldn't sleep. I was awake all night looking up every LDS article about pornography. It seemed to me that they mostly just talked about how we should avoid pornography or else it would become an addiction. There was nothing there for the wives. I started crying again. I wanted him to hear me and to know how bad he had hurt me. Hank would later reveal that he had viewed pornography every time he had used the computer while I was visiting family after New Year's. I would have never guessed this.

January through August, I was in denial. I didn't know the entire truth—that his pornography viewing had really increased when he was in graduate school. I believed that his recently confessed "slip-up" was a one-time event. I was constantly trying to figure out what I could do to not let the "slip-ups" happen again. I thought, *Well, he's doing the right things. He's reading his scriptures, so maybe it's my fault he's slipping up.* In the past, I had never gone that long reading my scriptures every day like he had. During this time in our marriage, I did read my scriptures faithfully, and I wrote in my journal every day. It now seems foolish for me to think that somehow by me doing these things every day I was going to stop my husband from looking at porn and masturbating. But it was the only thing that made sense to me. I thought that Hank would never lie to me. I thought that his honesty was the only thing we had going for us now. He would give me many minimal confessions that would make me feel that he was being open with me at this time. We had this system where every single night I'd ask him if he was sober and he would always say yes.

We bought him a ring that was a "don't look at porn" ring to help him remember. Looking back now I feel so sad about that time. I feel so bad for myself. I had no idea what was really going on that whole time. I was just doing the best I could with the information I had. A lot of times when I would forget to ask him at night how he had done that day, the next day I would call him right away because I would get so panicky. I had to make sure he hadn't looked at pornography. I thought that checking in with him was the only way he was going to stay sober. A lot of times, I would imagine the perfect situation of how I would react to it if he slipped up again. It is ironic that while he was fantasizing about women, I was fantasizing about what my reaction might be. It was so messed up.

He later told me that after he confessed his "slip-up" to me in January, he went for over three months without viewing pornography. In May, he went back to it again. We had put a better blocker on the computer, and this time he didn't know the password, but he inevitably found his way around it. A blocker is there to protect the innocent, and he's not innocent. I had just started a new job at the gym teaching gymnastics. I could take my son with me, so Hank was left home alone in the evening. That is when it all started up again. I still had no idea. I really didn't even worry about him being alone because I believed we had the perfect blocker in place. I was checking in with him every night to see if he was still sober; we had this new, better blocker on the computer; and this time he didn't know the password. I still trusted him and I didn't know he could take the blocker off. Now I find it interesting that he would always tell me to call him when I was on my way home from teaching gymnastics. I thought this was his way of checking up on me to make sure I was arriving home safely, but really it was to give him a heads-up so I didn't walk in on him viewing pornography.

I have a friend who was always talking to me about her husband who was a drug addict that constantly lied about his addiction. I would always say to Hank, "I can't believe he is lying about it." I would also make other shaming comments to him without realizing he was back to viewing pornography. When he wouldn't do the dishes, I would say, "Well, at least you aren't a drug addict." And when another friend told me her husband was struggling with a pornography problem, I said, "Can you believe he won't go confess to the bishop?" Those were the shame messages I would give to him during this time. I wonder if he ever thought, *I'm no better than these guys that my wife can't believe are acting the way they are.* One evening after talking to Hank about a traumatic event that happened in my friend's marriage, I turned to him and said, "I am so happy that we have such a good marriage." He said, "Yeah, we do." In hindsight, he was definitely not as enthusiastic about saying that as I was.

It was Thursday, August 1. I had just arrived home from work so excited because Hank had Friday off, and we had planned a fun weekend together. As I walked in the door Hank said, "I slipped up again." This time I did not see it coming, but because I had imagined to myself the perfect way I would react when it did happen, I felt like I reacted perfectly.

I immediately asked, "What did you look at? Did you masturbate too? Was Mason [our toddler-aged son] in the room?"

He answered "Yes, Mason was in the room when I masturbated."

I cussed at him, I threw things at him, and I threw all the dishes in the kitchen onto the floor. I was so proud of myself for reacting in such a drastic way. One reason I reacted differently this time was because my son was with him. The mother bear really came out in me. I told him there was no way our son was going to be exposed to pornography by his father. I continued slamming things even though Mason was asleep. I then went into our bedroom. He was already getting the air mattress out. Instead of crying this time, I became numb. I wanted to know what he had been looking at. I tried to find out how to retrieve deleted search histories. I didn't find anything. I looked all night long and then I tried setting up more blockers. I was numb, I was exhausted, and, oh yeah, I was also pregnant.

That next morning, I was thinking about my pregnant body. This wasn't the ideal body compared to what you would see with porn stars. I got out of the shower and looked in the mirror, and for the first time, I saw no flaws in my body. Here I was, the day after Hank confessed, yet I felt so beautiful. I knew it was God wanting me to see myself as He sees me. I realized that my beauty isn't dependent upon if I get ready for the day, what type of clothes I'm wearing, if I'm wearing make-up, what Hank thinks about me, or what he thinks about other women. It doesn't even matter what I think about me. I am beautiful. This was a tender mercy that the Lord blessed me with.

The Lord has given me other tender mercies that prepared me for the day Hank confessed everything. After Hank's "slip-up" in January,

I started doing a little more research on pornography addictions. I came across several blogs and articles that fascinated me and that I definitely used after Hank's full confession. I think in the end these resources saved our marriage. They talked about the importance of setting boundaries with someone who is addicted to pornography. So right after Hank confessed the second time, I sat down and wrote out a list of boundaries. I also told him that I expected him to do more than have a broken heart and contrite spirit every time he confessed and repented. He's done that all of his life. That's not enough to treat an addiction. I said, "You are going to do more than the spiritual things to recover. I expect you to attend 12-step meetings, go to therapy, and I need you to read the book *Rowboats and Marbles* along with the article "Detachment 180." I told him that I expected him to be honest with me, and if I ever caught him lying to me, I would kick him out of the house. I explained to him that while the Atonement heals over and over again, I'm only human. I can only take so much. Every time you act out, you do so at the risk of losing me.

After reading the book and the article I had suggested, Hank was prompted to write me a disclosure letter of *everything* he had ever done in regards to pornography. He e-mailed it to me while I was at work. Reading it made me sick to my stomach. I became physically ill. He had been lying about the severity of his addiction and the frequency of his viewing from day one. I started to panic because I realized that I had written the boundaries out last night and one was that if I ever found out he was lying to me I would kick him out. I felt like he'd been lying to me about really serious things for our entire marriage. We were in grad school, dirt poor, living in Georgia, and had no family that he could stay with. I started wondering if I would really be able to kick him out because of all the lies. I texted him back, "I got your e-mail. It made me sick to my stomach. I'd like to go to the temple tonight, so I'd like you to watch Mason. I'm taking all of the devices. And after that, I'd like you to leave the apartment." So I kicked him out! He was shocked. He started thinking, *I'm going to lose my family over this.*

He actually went camping the first night. I didn't even ask him where he stayed because I've always been the financial person, and I didn't know if he would go splurge on a fancy hotel room or something else. But he went camping instead, and it was in Georgia, and it was August. He was miserable. I was so glad he was miserable. The next night, he ended up getting a hotel. He stayed in the hotel for almost two weeks. The whole time, I didn't initiate anything. He had to do the initiating. The night I kicked him out, he printed out an online book that told about the experiences of a recovering pornography addict. He felt like it was the story of his own life. I kicked him out on Friday, and by Saturday morning, he'd read the entire book. On Sunday, he sent out an e-mail to both of our parents and all of his siblings telling them about his addiction, which was a huge step for him.

The separation was good for both of us. He hit rock bottom, and he would come over in the evenings to just talk and process. We only spent one or two hours together and we had really productive conversations. I wasn't crying in front of him anymore because I was detaching. I acted like "I don't need you" even though I was dying inside. He wrote another complete disclosure starting with the first time he acted out until the present. I think it was only because I was numb that I could handle it, otherwise it would have destroyed me. Normally, you would save disclosures like that to tell in front of a therapist and not go into as much detail. I was grateful for it though, because he didn't do any trickle disclosures. He did it all at once in a notebook that I was able to read. I felt like I needed to know what I was forgiving him for. It was terrible, horrible, disgusting. He wrote every website he'd been to, every girl he had searched, and he told me all of the weird things he had done. It was gross. While growing up, sexuality was a very hush-hush topic in his home. I knew that his parents never gave him the sex talk until he was at least fourteen. He figured things out on his own. The first time he masturbated, he didn't know what it was. He was so innocent about it. He even wrote about it in his journal, "the craziest thing happened to me." And of course when he found out masturbation was wrong he ripped that page out of his journal! He had no idea. As I read his full disclosure, I was so numb, and my only thought was, *Okay, he is really sick.* When he wrote that all out, I think it was good for him to realize that this was an addiction and it always had been. I think it also helped him because he told me everything. He let go of a lot of shame. It reinforced to him that he could say everything to me and I would still love him.

After my numbness wore off, everything caught up to me. I could barely function. My home quickly became a disaster. Dirty dishes were stacked in my sink for days while the cockroaches multiplied. I couldn't sleep. I had no appetite and lost over five pounds in my second trimester of pregnancy. I threw my toddler in front of the TV for more hours than I would like to admit. We were separated for two weeks. The first month after his disclosure we ate fast food almost every night and the second month we ate frozen food. We took out additional student loans to pay for my husband's sex addiction therapist. Anytime I talked to friends I would think, *If only you knew what my life was* really *like*. On the outside it seemed like I had everything together, but I felt like my life was falling apart.

Since then, something has clicked with Hank. Once I realized he had an addiction, things became more manageable. For some reason I couldn't deal with random slip-ups like we had had in January, but I could deal with an addiction. There are solutions for an addiction. There are no solutions for random slip-ups. I can't control that. I know I can't control an addiction either, and I know it's always going to be there, but it's a relief to know we can take steps toward recovery. Since that full disclosure, Hank's done everything right. It finally just clicked once he knew what he was dealing with. He's been going to bishops since he was twelve years old, trying to figure out how to stop. And all of a sudden, there were these other things. He went to five 12-step meetings a week. He started going to a really great therapist who focuses on sex additions, which was a miracle in itself that we found that particular one. He read all the literature about it that he could get his hands on. He has been committed to being well.

At this point we needed to address our physical intimacy. Hank always took care of me sexually, and so I thought we were okay in this area of our relationship. But in hindsight I can see that it all was very mechanical. I thought it was fine during that time because I didn't know any differently. I was really naïve to what pornography was and what he had actually been looking at. I just thought pornography was pictures of naked women. I didn't think it included videos. It is so sad in today's world that people see sexual acts before they even have sex themselves. While visiting his therapist, Hank was told to do a ninety-day sex fast. This was huge for us. The therapist helped us both realize that things we were doing sexually were actually very unhealthy for Hank's addiction and for me.

Hank's therapist told him that with any type of addiction there's a chemical reaction where the cravings for their drug or "fix" are stronger around days 30, 60, 90, 120, six months, and one year of their sobriety. When we did our sex fast, my husband definitely noticed a stronger temptation around those days, and he was more anxious and irritable. Plus he was learning how to deal with emotions that he hadn't paid attention to since his addiction started at age twelve. He was emotional a lot, and I felt like I was living with a twelve-year-old girl on her period. During our sex fast, my husband learned that his temptations were physiological and predictable and would pass after a couple of days. Obviously, his addiction was still triggered every day, but his cravings were stronger and felt more overwhelming during those times. Taking sex off the table also helped him focus on working through deeper emotions instead of focusing on when and how he was going to have sex next. Apparently porn addicts think about that often. I would say that our sex fast was vital to our recovery. My husband had no idea what healthy sexuality looked like because he has been an addict since he was twelve. I had no idea what healthy sexuality looked like because he had brought his porn addiction into our marriage. The fast helped us see the unhealthiness we didn't even realize was there. For him, the sex fast helped him reset his brain. The sex fast also helped us learn to connect in other ways and figure out what healthy sexuality even looked like. After the sex fast, sex has been a lot different for us. It was huge for him because he realized that sex was a want and not a need. For me it removed that pressure that I was constantly feeling. We had had sex nearly every day since we were married. All of a sudden that pressure was off of me.

For both of us, it was about learning to talk about things, to have more emotional and spiritual intimacy, and to learn how to touch in nonsexual ways. In the past, every time I'd hug or kiss him, I always knew what was coming next. It's been interesting to see this process unfold. After our sex fast was over I was eight months pregnant, and now we have a newborn. So our lives are different in general, and it's hard to know how much of this is the stage of life that we're in versus how much of it is the addiction. And even after the sex fast, I still wasn't quite sure what was healthy for us.

I have started attending a Baptist sex addiction recovery group—talk about a Southern experience! I meet with a group of women whose husbands are ex-pastors who got fired for looking at pornography. They all talk about Jesus and grace. They have all helped me learn about grace in a way I've never understood it before. It's not just, "If I accept Jesus, I'm saved." It's, "If I wake up knowing that I'm going to sin that day, I need His grace already. If I accept His grace, then I'll be connected, and I'll want to do His will." That's not their lingo, but it's similar to our doctrine. I've attended retreats with other LDS women who share their stories about living with pornography in their marriages. I'm also connected anonymously on Facebook with other women who are living with pornography in their marriages. Journaling has been huge for me, especially when everything first came out. My husband has been okay with me telling who I need to tell. I've told three or four of my really close friends. It turns out their husbands have porn problems too. I also do a phone-in 12-step meeting called Healing through Christ.

I have experienced my own miracles throughout this process. Right after Hank's disclosure, I was so traumatized and in such shock but I felt that I was blessed with some very sacred experiences. I truly had my own "Liberty Jail" moments.

I have learned to not feel responsible for my husband's salvation. I don't believe I've been perfect in my marriage, but one scripture has given me hope while living with pornography in my marriage. Back in January, when I didn't know how bad everything really was, I was reading Doctrine and Covenants 45:3–5: "Listen to him who is the advocate with the Father, who is pleading your cause before him—Saying: Father, behold the sufferings and death of him who did no sin, in whom though wast well pleased; behold the blood of thy Son which was shed, the blood of him whom though gavest that thyself might be glorified; Wherefore, Father, spare these my brethren that believe on my name, that they may come unto me and have everlasting life."

I pictured my Savior standing next to me and pleading, "Listen to me who is the advocate with the Father, who is pleading your husband's cause before you. Behold the sufferings and death of him who did no sin; behold the blood of your Savior which was shed. . . . Wherefore, spare your husband, that he may come unto me and have everlasting life."

After Hank's full disclosure, I was pondering this image in my mind. I had another, even more hopeful image come to my mind. I imagined myself standing next to my Savior, but this time I was united with Him. We were pleading my husband's cause together before our Heavenly Father. I said to Heavenly Father, "Listen to me, who is the wife of my husband, who is pleading his cause before Thee. Behold my sufferings, I who did no sin in my marriage, in whom Thou wast well pleased. Wherefore Father, spare my husband; that he may come with me and have everlasting life with me."

27

I hate when my husband is misunderstood. I feel like pornography addicts are culturally looked down upon or pitied as "sinners" and that it is their sins that led them to such a horrible habit. While often true, I also see pornography addicts as innocent ten-year-old boys home alone on the computer or curious teenagers unable to healthily process negative emotions, then fast forwarded ten, fifteen, twenty years or so into the future to see them as my husband. Pornography addicts are not just "sinners," like we all are, but people who are emotionally, mentally, and spiritually sick.

I also hate being misunderstood as the wife of a pornography addict. I didn't cause my husband's addiction, I can't cure it, and I can't control it. I am suffering from betrayal trauma and it is not my responsibility to "help" my husband get and stay sober. I am just as powerless over my husband's addiction as he is. It is only through God that my husband can maintain sobriety and recovery, and it is only through God that I can recover from the trauma I have experienced and that I continue to experience as I live with pornography in my marriage.

I recognize that my husband most likely will not be healed of his addiction in this life and he will have to actively work on recovery for the rest of his life. However, as I let this knowledge sink in the first few days after learning he had an addiction, the image of our Savior healing him kept coming to my mind. In 3 Nephi 17:7–10, Jesus says,

> Have ye any that are sick among you? Bring them hither. Have ye any that are lame, or blind, or halt, or maimed, or leprous, or that are withered, or that are deaf, or that are afflicted in any manner? Bring them hither and I will heal them, for I have compassion upon you; my bowels are filled with mercy. . . . I see that your faith is sufficient that I should heal you. And it came to pass that when he had thus spoken, all the multitude, with one accord, did go forth with their sick and their afflicted, and their lame, and with their blind, and with their dumb, and with all them that were afflicted in any manner; and he did heal them every one as they were brought forth unto him. And they did all, *both they who had been healed and they who were whole,* bow down at his feet, and did worship him; and as many as could come for the multitude did kiss his feet, insomuch that they did bathe his feet with their tears.[29]

It is an honor for me to fight alongside the man I love, who is sick with a pornography addiction, and who is working diligently to be in active recovery. I want to be by my husband's side in the next life when he is brought to our Savior and healed completely of his addiction. After all of the pain and heartache, the trauma, the sickness and hopelessness, after all of the triumph, joy, and happiness, and even recovery in this life, I want to be by my husband's side as we bathe our Savior's feet in our tears and worship Him and thank Him together. I hope and pray that my husband continues to choose to fight and work on his recovery. If he does, I know that we will experience more joy and happiness together in this life and in the life to come, more than we can even imagine. If my husband doesn't choose that, I know that I will still be okay because my life is in God's hands.

APPLYING BETRAYAL TRAUMA TO SARAH'S EXPERIENCE

Steffens and Means identified possible reasons why Sarah and women like her experience such incredible pain upon learning about their husband's pornography addiction. They stated,

> The depth and expectations of our deepest attachment bond, the piercing pain produced by betrayal trauma, the universal fear of abandonment generated by sexual betrayal, the threat of repeated incidents and the isolation and loneliness created by delayed emotional reconnection—provides part of the answer to [why discovering pornography can be so painful].[30]

Sarah's story illustrates the distress women feel when they experience betrayal trauma from their husband hiding secrets and locking them out of their innermost thoughts and emotions. Upon learning about their husband's pornography addictions, women experience shock, confusion, and sometimes an inability to function for months at a time. Like Sarah, they experience sleepless nights and even become physically sick once the sordid details of their husband's secret activities have been revealed.

In response to the trauma women experience, they might also exhibit a variety of codependent behaviors, such as taking it upon themselves to "fix" their husband by having sex with him every day, by monitoring his electronic devices, or by keeping track of his time when he is not with them. Women who have been traumatized by their husband's pornography use want to do everything they can to avoid the painful emotions of hearing about another incident of their husband's pornography use, so they try to do all in their power to keep their husband away from pornography. Women like Sarah desperately want to find emotional safety in their marital relationships, but for many of them this is seldom realized.

Women traumatized by their husband's pornography use will have emotional and spiritual needs that arise. Sarah articulates such needs, and like the other women we interviewed, she found comfort and solace through opening up to family members and trusted friends. These same women discovered hope in the prospect of recovering and healing by connecting with other women who are experiencing the same trauma and through the enabling power of the Atonement. Sarah, like all the women we interviewed, often cried out to God, wondering why He had forsaken her. However, they eventually realized that Heavenly Father had not only been with them throughout their entire "Liberty Jail" experience, He had also turned it into something sacred and personally instructive. Elder Jeffrey R. Holland has taught that the Lord is with us always, especially during the most miserable experiences of our lives. He is with us in the worst settings, while enduring the most painful injustices, and while facing the most insurmountable odds and opposition we have ever faced. Elder Holland said,

> In one way or another, great or small, dramatic or incidental, every one of us is going to spend a little time in Liberty Jail—spiritually speaking. We will face things we do not want to face for reasons that may not be our fault. Indeed, we may face difficult circumstances for reasons that were absolutely right and proper, reasons that came *because* we were trying to keep the commandments of the Lord. We may face persecution, we may endure heartache and separation from loved ones, we may be hungry and cold and forlorn. Yes, before our lives are over we may all be given a little taste of what the prophets faced often in their lives.
>
> But the lessons of the winter of 1838–39 teach us that every experience can become a redemptive experience if we remain bonded to our Father in Heaven through it. These difficult lessons teach us that man's extremity is God's opportunity, and if we will be humble and faithful, if we will be believing and not curse God for our problems, He can turn the unfair and inhumane and debilitating prisons of our lives into temples—or at least into a circumstance that can bring comfort and revelation, divine companionship and peace.[31]

The stories shared in this book will show how women have handled pornography in their marriages, and how eventually they were able to feel the profound love of their Heavenly Father as they discovered how intimately aware He was of their suffering.

2 DISCOVERY

The Spirit, voice
Of goodness, whispers to our hearts
A better choice
Than evil's anguished cries.[32]

         – "Our Savior's Love"

Wives are often deeply affected by their husband's pornography use, consequently, feelings of betrayal permeate all aspects of their lives. Many women feel that their husband's habitual pornography use can be considered virtual infidelity. At the same time, some women also recognize that an addiction is an illness and that their husband needs help in dealing with it. Clinicians have reported that when an individual discovers or rediscovers their partner's secret sexual behavior, such as pornography use, it is often a life-changing event. Steffens and Means said,

> All of us who've lived through the discovery of sexual betrayal remember in razor-sharp detail the agony, shock and overwhelming loss that ripped through our lives in that one earth-shattering moment in time. From that moment on we instinctively knew nothing would ever be the same again.[33]

Women we interviewed reported an array of emotions ranging from numbness to rage. Their emotions ricocheted all over when they learned about their husband's pornography use. At the end of this chapter, Alice's story describes her experience learning about her husband's pornography use after they had been married for seven years. In Alice's case, the feelings of betrayal were exacerbated by the fact that her own parents knew the truth and did not tell her. The trauma of learning about the pornography addiction and the lies that have been told causes intense fear and uncertainty for most wives.

Clinicians who work with women experiencing betrayal trauma have identified two types of reactions to the trauma—fight or flight. These two types of reaction are found in a response to any intense fear. Dr. Skinner described what fight and flight look like in women when they are reacting to learning about their husband's pornography use.

> The "fight" is the anger, the irritability, and the screaming at others. These emotions sometimes really scare the women and their spouse because now they are being angry in ways they or their husband have never seen before. The husband is wondering, *Why is she so upset? I* have seen situations where women actually throw things. They have done things that realistically could be considered physical abuse (e.g., women hitting, punching, and pulling hair of their husband). This is an extreme manifestation of this, but it is not uncommon.
>
> This kind of emotional reaction is very uncomfortable for many of the women because it is not common for them to feel that kind of intensity. Now they are looking at themselves and asking, *What is wrong with me? Why am I acting in this way?* If her husband uses her emotional reaction against her by saying something like, "Look, if you could just calm down and we could talk about this," this can create a fracture in the relationship.
>
> The flight comes about in the emotional disconnect from women's own emotions, and the emotions of others. The manifestation of this is when women stop talking to their friends, run from relationships that used to be close to them, and emotionally disconnect from the world around them. There is also a flight away from the relationship where women stop opening up, where they just trudge through the emotions where there is not anything but a shell of her former self. In the flight, what you start to see is a person who feels a deep sense of sadness and loneliness, and they just don't know where to go with it. They feel stuck. They are not reaching out to people anymore and their social relationships aren't what they used to be. On top of that, they don't trust their spouse so they aren't opening up to him. They might have family members saying that something is wrong, and so they ask, but because women don't want to spill the beans they bite their tongue and

they end up not saying anything at all. Women often find themselves in this state of isolation. They keep themselves away from any kind of support that they could have had.

IS PORNOGRAPHY VIRTUAL INFIDELITY?

Christian author William M. Struthers wrote, "The viewing of pornography and sexually acting out may not meet the letter of the law for adultery (Matthew 5:28), but it certainly meets the spirit of the law."[34] Many women that we interviewed felt that their husband's habitual pornography use was virtual infidelity. When we asked Dr. Skinner if many of his female clients consider viewing pornography as infidelity, he said:

> Some women do and others don't. There is no fixed answer for that one. Some people absolutely feel like it is infidelity and others say, "No, that's pornography. I consider it different because he is not connecting with other women." If women are connected to their spouse and if they know his history and background, they may be less likely to view it as infidelity. For example, if a wife knows that her spouse has dealt with this problem since he was age eleven and if he has been at least somewhat open with her, then that is different than if he has kept it a secret and hasn't told her anything about it. If a couple has been married for fifteen years, and now all of a sudden the husband discloses that he has this problem and has hidden it from his wife for all of those years, that is much more intense. So, part of it depends on the openness, the vulnerability, and the communication in a relationship. It really boils down to the same fundamental communication questions of, "Can we talk?" "Are we open with each other?" "Are we honest with each other?" And maybe the real crux of the relationship is that when it comes to the deceit and the lying then it sends a message that "You don't really know me."
>
> I think it feels more like infidelity when there is not a discussion or disclosure about what a husband's pornography use means. My experience is that women often go to what I call the worst-case scenario thinking. Women worry about other things that he hasn't told them. If they have been lying and hiding things then women question, "What else have you not been telling me?" She may be making it worse in her mind than it actually is. Because of the unknown, her mind may think, *Could it be this?* or *Who is this guy? What is this actually all about?*

There are additional factors that can exacerbate the trauma of learning about a husband's pornography addiction. Some women told us that they sensed something was not right in the marriage or with their husband for quite a long time prior to learning about his pornography use. When women confronted their husbands, the husbands would often deny that there was a problem. Women also reported that their husbands would minimize or justify their pornography use. Some women also shared their frustration about the invisibility of using pornography, which allowed their husband's pornography use to continue undetected. Some women felt their husband's secretive pornography use and denial upon confrontation allowed their husband an opportunity for "crazy-making"—when one person, in this case the husband, suggests that the wife's perception is inaccurate, when in actuality, her perception is precisely accurate.[35] Crazy-making seems to exacerbate the trauma experienced by women. Finally, almost all women told us how when they learned of the pornography use, they wondered why they were not "enough" for their husband and blamed themselves for their husband's pornography use.

INTUITION THAT SOMETHING'S WRONG

Before learning that their husband was using pornography, most women we interviewed intuitively knew that something was wrong in their marriage, even though they had minimal or no concrete evidence to support their belief. Sometimes this feeling persisted for months or years before learning of the pornography problem. This intuition may cause a wife to question her husband in order to find answers. Alice shared with us her intuition that something was wrong for a long time, even in the face of her husband's denials. She said:

> When I started having suspicions that something wasn't quite right in our marriage, I would just blame it on the insecurities that stemmed from my eating disorder or something coming more from my side of the relationship. There was just some kind of a disconnect and emptiness. There was something missing, and I couldn't put my finger on it. We never fought a lot, but we weren't connecting on a spirit-to-spirit level. I always blamed myself. I think that women do that naturally, and women with eating disorders certainly do that naturally. I would talk to him about it and say, "Do you think there is something missing? Do you think we need to spend more time together?" He would grab me, hold me, love me, and say that it was probably just my eating

disorder making me feel this way. Afterward, I would think to myself, *I am such a jerk. What is my problem? Everything is fine.* He totally capitalized on my weaknesses, but it always seemed to make perfect sense to me. *Of course it was me.* So I would apologize for asking him if something was going on and then be on my merry way, thinking of how lucky I was to have such a forgiving husband. He is so patient and so loving. That conversation happened over and over before I knew pornography was a problem.

Ashley shared with us how she knew something was wrong in her marriage, but Michael denied that anything was wrong:

> Before Michael came clean [about his pornography addiction], we argued a lot because I knew something was wrong but he kept denying it. I asked him so many times, because I really felt like he was viewing pornography, but he blew it off and even accused me of being the crazy one. Before his confession, the spirit in our home was dark. I turned to other things, such as yoga and Native American traditions. I was so desperate to have a good spirit in our home that I tried different ways to cleanse our home of these awful feelings. There was a lot of anger. There were times I didn't even want to come home. I felt happier and more spiritual at work with my students, because I at least had their respect.

If women sensed that something was wrong with their husbands or in their marriage and those concerns were minimized, ignored, or attributed to women's own problems, learning the truth about pornography use can cause women to feel a great sense of betrayal.

THE RELATIONSHIP FRACTURE

Another problematic scenario for women is whether they knew their marital relationship was compromised or not before disclosure day. In other words, was there already a fracture in the relationship leading up to the disclosure, or did the wife believe that everything was fine? According to Dr. Skinner, it is more traumatizing to the woman if she believed all along that the marriage was fine.

> The relationship fracture comes in at least two versions. One version is that the marital relationship has already had the fracture, and there are already marital problems. Another is that everything was going okay until discovery day, and then the fracture occurs. Sometimes there is a lead up to it, but other times women are caught

completely off guard. They think that things are going well and they really are not. I believe in most instances that the fracture occurs before the discovery day.

In my experience, it is more often that the woman doesn't know about the man's pornography use. She discovers it and that is incredibly traumatizing because she thought things were okay. Then she feels stupid. She is wondering, *What is wrong with me? Why didn't I see this?* And then if she looks over the past, she starts realizing that there were symptoms that she didn't see. That can be very confusing to her.

MINIMIZATION OR DENIAL OF PORNOGRAPHY

Many women we interviewed reported that their husbands either denied that they had a pornography problem or that they completely minimized the extent of the problem. Many husbands continue to deny or lie about pornography after the initial disclosure. Lying and avoiding the consequences of lying become almost instinctual for someone who is addicted to any substance, including pornography. Floyd P. Garrett, a behavioral medicine psychiatrist, had this to say about an addict's lying:

> The first casualty of addiction, like that of war, is the truth. At first the addict merely denies the truth to himself. But as the addiction, like a malignant tumor, slowly and progressively expands and invades more and more of the healthy tissue of his life and mind and world, the addict begins to deny the truth to others as well as to himself. He becomes a practiced and profligate liar in all matters related to the defense and preservation of his addiction, even though prior to the onset of his addictive illness, and often still in areas as yet untouched by the addiction, he may be scrupulously honest.[36]

Deception is a skill many pornography addicts have mastered. Struthers stated,

> Whether through direct lies of commission (stating falsehoods), omission (only telling part of the truth), or assent (remaining silent and allowing the silence to be interpreted as innocence), deception is a skill that many men [with addictions] have honed as part of their descent into depravity. Unfortunately, this skill is so well practiced on others that a man may effectively deceive himself with respect to his motives, frequency of use, and the depth to which his pornography problem has developed.[37]

Linda Hatch, a certified addiction therapist, states that sex addicts, including pornography addicts, "try to avoid feeling *shame*. They also know on some level that others would disapprove of their addictive behaviors. In order to keep the feelings of guilt and shame at bay, addicts find ways to minimize, rationalize, or justify their behavior. In so doing they build up a layer of denial, [which magnifies the weight of the shame]."[38]

Reid and Gray identified another reason men may feel lying about their pornography use is acceptable. Men may feel they are being altruistic by protecting others, especially their wives, from the truth. In reality, Reid and Gray indicate that this is a rationalization some people use to justify not telling their spouse. Some people rationalize procrastinating a disclosure because they want to avoid hurting their spouses. This ignores the fact that dishonesty is as serious as the behavior itself. Avoiding hurting a spouse can simply be an excuse to protect oneself from a spouse's reaction and the consequences of one's behavior. As a result, many individuals chose to continue indulging in pornography while keeping it a secret.[39]

Melanie's quote below illustrates how painful it is when a husband reveals his pornography use. She shared with us how heart-breaking it is with each new confession, particularly when deception is involved.

> We just had an experience on Monday where we had been discussing things, and I asked him how long he had been sober. I thought it had been at least three months, but he said, "No." This was hard for me to understand because I would ask him and he would say yes, he had been sober. But he was always referring to that very day that I asked him. I was asking if he had been sober since the last time I had asked him. At this point, he said, "No, it has been about three weeks." This broke my heart all over again. I just need to find the right way to respond, because it still breaks my heart every time.

Susan explained how her husband minimized his pornography use and always tried to justify it:

> When I would confront my husband he would say, "Oh, it's not that bad" and "It's not that big of deal." Then I would say, "Really, you do that? Like how often?" He would reply, "Well, more than I should, probably." Then I would reply, "And you don't think that it's a problem?" If I asked him point blank, he wasn't one that would habitually lie, but he minimized. He would also justify it by telling me, "Well, I

didn't pay for it." I told him, "I don't care if you paid for it; you're still watching it! It's not about the money!" He just wouldn't outright lie to me. Instead, he would minimize or try to justify. But it was never a bold-faced lie. He never came right out and told me, "No, I haven't looked at anything."

Some addicts might actually confess to doing something, but the confession is merely a ruse to make his wife think he is being honest with her. Alice told us that her husband "would make up fake confessions, because he knew that if he told me he was fine, I wouldn't believe him and I would be suspicious."

Whether the lie was a minimization, a half-truth, or a bold-faced lie, most people feel betrayed when they have been lied to, especially by their spouse. The trauma of being betrayed may become an ingrained part of a marriage if deception happens over and over again. After catching sexual addicts in a lie, especially repeated lies, it is natural to wonder if the spouse was ever truthful on any topic.[40]

INVISIBILITY OF PORNOGRAPHY USE

Some women may never catch their husbands in the actual act of viewing pornography. There is typically no physical evidence or definitive indicator that your husband has been looking at pornography. It is easier to recognize when someone has been drinking alcohol or using crack or heroin, but it is much more difficult to recognize when someone is entrenched in a pornography problem.[41] The women we interviewed shared the frustration they felt in regards to this invisibility of pornography use. Amber commented,

> At least with a drug addict, you can give a urine test or blood test to see if they have been using, but with a porn addict you can never know for sure if and when they have been using. All you have is their word, and up to this point in our marriage, Luke's word has meant nothing. He did pass the polygraph test that I made him take after he came out of treatment, but they only asked him three questions. The main question they asked him was if he had been completely honest with me in his disclosure. I think I will have him take a polygraph test every year just so I know if he is using pornography, which is invisible to me.

Ashley shared this same view:

> Pornography is not like drugs. You can't tell if your husband is sober or not. You are not losing money because of it and you can't tell if he is going through withdrawals. It's not like he's hiding illegal substances. It is just right there on his phone or computer, easily accessed by the touch of a button.

The invisibility of pornography contributes to feelings of betrayal and makes establishing trust extremely difficult. This makes it tricky for women to know when they should believe their husbands. The invisibility of pornography use or other sexual behaviors leaves spouses with "no concrete evidence and thus no way to prove what they only fear."[42]

CRAZY-MAKING

During the interviews, we frequently heard the term "crazy-making," where one spouse's view of what is real is constantly undermined (overtly or covertly) by their trusted partner in often subtle and imperceptible ways. People who constantly have their perceptions of reality denied by their spouse can lose their ability to see what is real, thus questioning whether their own mental health is to blame for the problems.[43] Because pornography use is invisible, it can easily be used for crazy-making in a marriage. Some women we interviewed wondered if they were losing their minds before they knew about their husband's pornography problem. They felt disconnected from their husbands and became very unsure of their own abilities to make proper assessments of others' behavior. Ashley described her experience:

> Michael had plenty of chances to tell me. I asked him so many times if he was viewing pornography because I really felt like he was, but he would blow it off and even accuse me of being the crazy one. He had so many chances to come clean and start the recovery process earlier. It would not have been so damaging to our relationship. I felt crazy. I felt that there was something going on, but he would always deny it. He would say, "Oh, it's just your emotions, you're being hormonal." I always felt like it was something I was doing.

Amber said,

> I asked Luke all the time, "Is there a problem?" because my gut always said that there was something not quite right about our

relationship. When I would ask him he would say, "Amber, you are creating something in your head that isn't real. Everything is really okay. This is not that big of deal. You act as if you want something to be wrong. You always want to pick a fight. You are always trying to find something wrong and there is nothing there." He was the master of manipulation and very convincing. He would always take the spotlight off himself and turn it on me. The next thing I knew, I would be the one apologizing for something I wasn't wrong about. I was convinced that there was something seriously wrong with me. My husband did a lot of crazy-making. I often wondered to myself if I was losing my mind. I would say that I knew there was something going on and he would assure me there wasn't. He would even make up events he would say happened that really didn't. I often wondered to myself if I was indeed losing my mind. After one incident of me accusing him that something was wrong and him denying it and making me feel like I was the crazy one, I apologized to him and in all sincerity asked him to check me in to a hospital because I really thought I was losing my mind. He said, "Well, where is the closest one?" He was more than willing to let me take the blame for this. I went as far as seeking counseling for myself because I was worried that there really was something wrong with me.

When husbands frame their spouse as the "crazy" one and later pornography use is discovered, the sense of betrayal is real. He has not only been secretly looking at pornography but he has lied about it, twisted the truth, and made his wife feel like she is the one who is out of touch with reality.

WOMEN BLAME THEMSELVES OR FEEL INADEQUATE

One of the most troubling aspects of a husband's pornography addiction is how detrimental it is to his wife and her perception of herself. In the interviews, all too often the wife blamed herself for her husband's addiction or felt that if she was somehow different from who she was, pornography wouldn't be a problem for her husband. This type of thinking is incredibly damaging to women. It can be very difficult to repair how a woman thinks about herself, especially if pornography use continues in her marriage. There were many moments, especially when pornography use had just been disclosed or re-disclosed, that women truly believed that if only they were more beautiful, thin, sexy, or intelligent, their husband would not have turned to pornography. Cynthia, a beautiful and loving mother of four boys, shared this with us:

As a woman, I think I am naturally inclined to doubt my self-worth. I have very negative feelings about my body. Pornography has served to confirm all of my doubts. I am definitely not the perky, firmed-tummy eighteen-year-old girl that I used to be, and certainly not the same girl he has seen thousands of times in videos and pictures. I wasn't that girl for very long in our marriage because I started having kids pretty quickly. So with all the sagginess that comes from having multiple children, it is real easy to think that I am not what he wants anymore.

Melanie explained the difficulty she had understanding her husband's pornography use and her pain. She said, "I still take it so personally. It still hurts so much. It is always in the back of my mind that he went to another source."

Sometimes other individuals unfamiliar with a pornography addiction mistakenly assume that the wives bear some responsibility for the problem. They may think and even advise women to lose some weight, dress up more often, or have sex more often as one way of addressing their spouse's pornography use. This advice can further traumatize a woman whose thoughts have already been along the lines of *If I was only different, he wouldn't have had to go to pornography.* In reality, the pornography addiction has nothing to do with a spouse.

Alice's story illustrates the betrayal trauma she experienced and factors that exacerbated her trauma. She had a sense that something was not quite right while her husband's pornography use remained invisible to her. In her story, a lot of crazy-making occurred. Her husband, Shawn, lied or minimized the problem for seven years. She felt deeply inadequate and insecure once she knew about Shawn's pornography addiction.

ALICE'S STORY

When Shawn asked me out on our first date, he was a freshman in college and I was a senior in high school. I remember thinking that there was no way that this really could be happening. He was the only boy in the whole world I had ever had a crush on. He was the student body president at our high school. He was good at sports, drama, and musicals. I was completely smitten. Right then I just thought this kid was my whole world. When we got married, he was a returned missionary and a worthy priesthood holder, and I had no idea that he had an issue with pornography.

I have an eating disorder that I have struggled with since I was twelve years old. I told Shawn everything about it from the beginning. I even made him attend therapy with me so he would know exactly what he was getting himself into.

In January 2007, we moved to Nevada. We had two boys at the time. We were both so excited to start this new adventure of moving away from where we had grown up. He had found a great job there, so I didn't even hesitate to move. But before we moved, my sister, who was seventeen years old, pregnant, and a recovering meth addict, had asked me to think about adopting her baby. I reluctantly told her I would consider it, but I really did not have any intention of doing it. I remember shaking my fist to Heavenly Father, saying, "I am not doing this—this is absolutely crazy." I asked Shawn about his feelings about the adoption. I told him that this is something you don't just jump on your wife's coattails and do. This is something that we really need to pray about and come to know for ourselves if it is what the Lord wants us to do. Shawn agreed. Looking back, I guess this is what scared him into going in and talking to the bishop. He knew he needed to clean up his life to receive this revelation for himself and his family. I guess it had to take something as big as adopting a baby to get him to confess his addiction, because otherwise I never would have found out. Shawn had become so good at hiding his addiction. I never imagined that he could lie to me. He was supposed to be the spiritual one. He was such a proactive member of the Church. He diligently served in several callings and he was so adamant that we were to church twenty minutes early every Sunday so we could sit on the soft seats.

I call disclosure day "D-Day." This is the day I found out about Shawn's pornography use and addiction. "D-Day" was July 5, 2007. I got a knock on our door that evening. I had just put the kids down for bed. When I opened the door, there stood a man in a suit. I was still so new to the ward, but I recognized him as either my bishop or a member of my bishopric. He kind of let himself in, and I was thinking that was weird because normally they want to make sure another priesthood holder is in the house before coming inside. I didn't know what to call him, and I wasn't sure if my husband had arranged this visit or not, so I just said, "Come on in!" But it was still weird the way he just walked in, so I hurried and said. "Well, Shawn is here." I really didn't know why he was there. I then started thinking he was there to talk to us about adopting my sister's baby. Shawn came around the corner and it was obvious that he knew the man in the suit was coming, and I still had no idea for sure who he was. We all sat down in the front room. I remember that the man in the suit was just kind of sitting in the corner away from us. It was the weirdest thing, because he was totally outside our range of communication. The man didn't say anything and Shawn sat down next to me and started getting really emotional. He then pulled out a letter and said, "There is something I need to share with you." In my mind, I am still thinking about the man in the suit. "Is he my bishop?" I was feeling so embarrassed because I had no idea who he was, and I felt like I was supposed to know him.

Anyway, Shawn pulled out his letter and he proceeded to confess everything about his pornography use; I mean *everything*. I had no idea, *absolutely* no idea. Sure, we had our problems; sure, I had noticed a disconnect in our marriage. I also knew that no marriage was perfect, but this was absolutely the *last* thing I suspected. He had never been mean to me or mistreated me, so I really had no reason to suspect that this was even going on. He proceeded to read the letter. In it he said that he had struggled with pornography from the time he was twelve years old, which is funny because that is the same time my eating disorder started. He just didn't think he needed to tell me about it before we were married because a lot of addicts, especially LDS addicts, who don't have sex before they're married think that once they get married and have sex, the addiction will just go away. He was actually able to stay sober the first nine months of our marriage. Unexpectedly, I became pregnant nine months into our marriage, and the thought of having to support a family must have triggered the addiction again.

When Shawn read the letter to me, I remember being emotionless, and he was just sobbing. He couldn't even breathe because he was sobbing so hard. I think I just didn't really understand what he was telling me. I know now I was in shock, but every once in a while I would look over at this strange man in a suit and wonder who in the world he was. I just kept listening and then looking at him. Listening and looking. Now that I have put everything in place, I realize that Shawn had gone to the bishop and told him everything. Shawn decided to write a letter to me to tell me about him using pornography. He told the bishop he was just going to leave it on my car. The bishop thought that would not be a great idea, so he was there to support Shawn in making sure he gave me the letter at an appropriate time and in the right way. Shawn had wanted to tell me earlier but didn't know how. The letter just covered the outline of his addiction.

I don't really even remember all that it said. I don't even know if I still have the letter. I have done a lot of burning since that day. Did you know that lingerie lights up like no other?

Shawn finished reading the letter and looked up at me. I looked at him and said, "Wow! That must have been really hard for you to do." I looked over at the man in the corner and then I said, "I need to go outside." It was 120 degrees outside, but that did not matter. I went over to Shawn and just hugged him. He was so broken and I didn't know what else to do. I really wasn't angry at this point. I grabbed my cell phone and headed outside for some fresh air. Shawn saw me grab my phone and so he said, "I probably should tell you that your mom, your dad, your sister, and your therapist in Utah already know about this." This was the biggest atomic bomb for me. He told me that they had known for five years. This was unbelievable to me. I think I decided right then that nobody was trustworthy. I was so upset and so numb that I just sat at the end of my driveway. It was the hottest day of the year and I just sat there. I kept wondering how my family could know for so long and not tell me. I have the best relationship with my dad. We have always been so close. I couldn't believe that he would keep this from me. My dad had been a bishop and my mom was a therapist. What were they thinking? This was absolutely unbelievable to me.

In the past, my sister had lived with us and had caught my husband looking at pornography. The poor thing didn't even know what to do or say. He told her that I knew about it and that we were working on it. It is unbelievable to me that she lived with us for six months and I lived with him all these years, and she caught him but I never did. I'm actually glad that I didn't catch him like so many wives do. I would always be afraid that he would just be going through the motions of getting better, not really wanting to get better, and all the while trying to convince me that he wanted to be better. My parents regret that they never told me. My dad has since said several times that there is no excuse for him keeping it from me. He should have told me.

After D-Day, we went straight into the Life Star program (an addiction recovery program). He would confess to me on a weekly basis, and I would put my feelings aside and actually honor him for confessing. He thought I was amazing, but inside I was dying. I kept thinking to myself, *If only I were prettier or skinnier. What is wrong with me, why am I not enough?* I resented Shawn and I was angry at God. In my eyes, I had done everything right. I dressed modestly, I was clean and pure, and I was naïve—everything you are supposed to be when you get married. I had been so honest with him about my eating disorder. Why didn't he tell me about his pornography problem? This was all beyond my belief. I would look up to heaven and say, "How could you let this happen to me?" I interpreted the teachings of my childhood to mean that if I lived righteously, I wouldn't have these types of trials. I truly believed that if I followed the yellow brick road, I would live happily ever after. Instead, Shawn and I had become the perfect storm. Here I was with an eating disorder caused from low self-esteem and a negative body image, and he was looking at pornographic women and lusting after their perfect bodies. I was riding on a storm-tossed sea and had no one to turn to for help.

Because Shawn had told my family, I never talked to them about it. I felt like they had chosen their side, and it was his. I really thought that I could fix him. I believed that if we had sex all the time that I could kill his sex drive and he wouldn't have any need to view pornography. That was my first phase: I could fix him. I needed to make this better because I was blaming myself for it.

I held on so tight for that first year after his disclosure, but I couldn't hold on any longer. It was just too much. I had stopped listening to myself. I had shut off my own brain and told myself that I would do whatever the bishop and my therapist told me. They told me to have more sex with him and this would help. They counseled me to read my scriptures more and say my prayers. When he tells you that he has relapsed, don't freak out on him but instead say, "That must have been so hard for you; thank you for being honest with me." They would say, "You don't want to scare him away from being honest." I owned his problem. I believed that if I wasn't nice to him he would never be honest with me, he would never get well, and it would be my fault. This type of thinking was so damaging to me.

In a few months, I finally had to leave my children and go to inpatient care for my eating disorder. I stopped living, I stopped eating, and my liver started failing. I lost twenty-five pounds in forty-five days and I just couldn't take the pain of his addiction anymore. He did tell me at one point that he was not stronger than the pornography addiction and that he could not overcome it. That was too much for me. He said, "I'm telling you this because this is going to be part of our lives forever, and you need to decide if you are going to stay or go." I told him that, to be honest, I couldn't do this. Something inside of me broke right there. I simply gave up and I stopped eating. It is obvious now that this was my trigger. Later on, I realized that he is not the one that made me stop eating. The choice for me was always there.

It was in the inpatient treatment center that I realized that I could not fix him. I also realized that if I proceeded in this manner, it was going to kill me. I learned that I can support him and love him, but I can also be mad at him, throw things at him, and even break things. He still has to be accountable for his choices and for his honesty with me. When I returned home from inpatient treatment, I was so angry. I was angry all the time. He would come home from work happy and feeling great because he had been sober for a while, and I would still be so mad. He wouldn't ever respond to my anger, so then I would be mad at myself for being mad at him. At this point I think everything had finally soaked in. I just couldn't believe that he had done this to me for so long and without my knowledge. Everything had become too hard, so one day I took it out on the wall, and I punched a hole right through it. My dad was so proud of me. He said that I truly was a redhead. I never was that kind of girl, but I am now!

The problem with my situation is that I never caught him in a lie. Some women whose husbands view pornography are so intense in patrolling their husbands that they put a GPS in their husband's car. I knew that if I started down that path that it would totally suck me in, so I never did it. But for me those times that I would say, "I feel like you need to tell me something about using pornography," and he would answer, "No, I'm fine," never felt right. I really didn't have any other evidence so I thought, "Well, life goes on." He had lied to me for seven years. I never had the closure that would come from him denying it and then me catching him by reviewing his search history on the computer. I never caught him, so I was left to my own devices to determine if he was lying to me or not. You just start making yourself crazy. Other women in my support group also say this has happened to them. At one point or another we all have questioned if we were losing our minds.

In 2009 we got a new bishop and Shawn relapsed totally. Not only did he relapse, but he was lying again. Everything was a lie. I never went the route of checking his e-mails. We had installed filtering software on the computer, and I told him that my house would be safe. He could go down the street and look at the neighbor's computer, but this house would be safe. He found ways around the software. I knew that something was wrong and that he was really struggling. I told him that I knew he had messed up royally and that I was not forgiving him. I felt so disconnected from him. I just wasn't moving past this the way I should be. He gave me a big hug and lovingly told me that maybe I should go talk to the bishop about this. Come to find out, he had been telling the bishop about his relapses but not telling me. Shawn wanted *me* to go to the one person that knew he had relapsed and talk to him about forgiveness. I made the appointment and while talking to the bishop, he kept saying, "Now Shawn is the one that suggested you come talk to me, right? You came because Shawn wanted you to? Alice, he is lying to you, so why would he send you in here to talk to me about forgiveness?" We both were stunned. The bishop didn't know what to say. I really needed some direction. There was not a good spirit in our house. The kids felt it and I felt it. I knew I couldn't forgive him overnight, and I felt stuck in my anger. I felt angry every time I was around him. Something had to give.

We had planned a family trip to LEGOLAND California for January 2010. In December 2009, I told him that I couldn't go. I am the type of mom that doesn't want to miss out on anything with her kids, but I knew I could not go with him. I was still so mad at him. I think it kind of shocked him that I was still struggling so much. When they came back from LEGOLAND he told me that all of 2009, he had been back into his addiction and had been lying about it. I just looked at him and I knew that if I was going to get any clarity in my life, I needed to be away from him. I felt like I was going under, but this time it was not eating disorder–related. I felt like my life was full of so much fog and mist that I needed to clean up or I was just going to keep floundering. I needed him to be gone. I would have these eight-hour breaks from him while he was at work where I would calm myself down and start feeling at peace, and then he would come home and the darkness and anger would start all over again. I constantly lived in fear of a confession that would shake my world. I couldn't live like that. I couldn't enjoy my kids. I guess the best way to describe it is that I just couldn't breathe. I was suffocating. I hate to use the word *control* because it is so attached to eating disorders, but I had no control in my life. I had given him all the power. He alone had the power to ruin my life and make it a living hell or make it wonderful. By nature, I am a happy person. I needed to remember how to get that back, so I told him that we needed a break. I told him he needed to go.

We were separated for about eight months. He was so mad that I was serious about this. He loved his kids, but he became someone that I didn't even know. When we separated, Shawn told the kids, "Daddy has to go away for a little while because he has not been telling the truth, he was telling too many lies, and he has to go somewhere to learn how to be honest." He didn't pack his stuff for two weeks because he didn't think I really meant it. He knew I was not one to make empty threats, but he just thought that there was no way I was going to go through with it. I think the reason I could go through with it was because it wasn't a punishment. It wasn't to hurt him—it was to *save* myself! That was why it stuck, because I needed to save myself. While we were separated, it went from things being okay, to really ugly, and then to really good.

During the separation, I started feeling empowered. I realized I do have choices in my life. I don't have to live waiting for disclosure after disclosure. I was living in constant fear, and even in the good times pornography was always in the back of my mind. I wouldn't let myself really enjoy anything because I always questioned if it was even real. I was so afraid of the fall that I thought would inevitably come, that I decided to just hate everything and remain miserable. I didn't realize that this is what I was doing until I got away from him. With him gone, I could finally get a long enough break from him to breathe again and heal. For me, being separated saved my life. It helped me find me again. It reminded me that I was in control of my own happiness. I could determine how things would go. I could tell him to sleep on the couch for a week. I became too comfortable with the separation. He hated it, and I am so glad that he hated it. That was a bonus. I had finally accepted things the way they were and not the way I thought they were supposed to be. We got back together the summer of 2010.

I have known about Shawn's addiction for seven years, and it has only been the last year and a half that he has really started into recovery. That is so sad, because I think to myself, *What has he been doing for five years? What a waste.* He always had one foot in and one foot out because he wasn't committed to being well. He finally decided to embrace recovery. He has been sober for over a year. I say that not really knowing if he is telling the truth, but my instincts are telling me that he is being honest.

He is learning to think differently about life. He is, for the first time, discovering what intimacy really means and what human connection is. He had never been intimate with me emotionally or spiritually. He never knew how to do that. He is learning not to objectify me and other women and he is discovering that we are equal. I am not his toy, and I am not his little pet. I am his wife.

Every time Shawn opened his mouth I was waiting for the worst to happen all over again. I would panic. A year and a half ago, I sat down with my therapist and told her that I was still struggling and I didn't even know where to start. There were so many different aspects of my life that were a mess. I went on and on talking about all that I have been through with my eating disorder and my husband's pornography addiction. Toward the end of the session I added, "For your information, I also have a daughter with cerebral palsy and a son who was just diagnosed with a mild form of Asperger's syndrome." Her jaw dropped. She could not believe that these were my FYIs. However, the trauma of my husband's pornography addiction and his lies outweighs all of them.

Now that I realize the extent of everything, I am in mourning. I mourn the loss of what I thought my marriage was, what I thought it was supposed to be, and also what it will never be. I have hopes that someday it can be great again, but it will never be what I wanted it to be. I can never pretend this didn't happen, and I will never be the same naïve girl. I never had trust issues before this. I never believed that human beings would purposely hurt each other, but now, that has all changed.

ALICE'S STORY AND LEARNING ABOUT A PORNOGRAPHY PROBLEM

Alice's story illustrates the trauma women experience when they learn about their husband's pornography addiction and the distress they experience as they live with pornography in their marriage. Like Alice, many women we interviewed had an intuition that something was wrong in their marriage for many years before learning about their husband's long-term pornography use. They too were subject to their husband's crazy-making tactics, which worsened their already existing insecurities. The invisibility of pornography use and the ongoing lies, either outright or more subtle minimizations of pornography, caused each woman continued traumatization. Many women questioned if their husbands still loved them, why they weren't enough to satisfy him sexually, and wished they were somehow different—perhaps skinnier or more beautiful. Alice's eating disorder caused her to wonder about her physical appearance prior to the disclosure, but her doubts about her appearance intensified after she learned about Shawn's pornography use. Although the other women we interviewed did not have eating disorders, doubts about their own physical appearance also intensified, their trauma started, and they too were left facing a future full of fear and uncertainty.

3 LOSS OF SELF

A conviction that you are a daughter of God gives you a feeling of comfort in your self-worth. It means that you can find strength in the balm of Christ. It will help you meet the heartaches and challenges with faith and serenity.[44]

– James E. Faust

The previous chapters have identified the challenges women face when they discover their husband's pornography use. After discovery, though, there is an extended period of time where women question themselves, their marriages, and even their spiritual beliefs and feelings. These topics will be covered in this chapter and the following two chapters. In this chapter, we will share the questions women ask about themselves about who they are, who their husband really is, and what the reality of their marriage is and actually has been.

Each of us constructs a personal identity in which we define who we are as we interact with others in our daily activities and roles. This identity is primarily developed during adolescence and the early adult years through a largely unconscious process of considering (a) who we have been in the past, who we are right now, and what we expect to be like in the future; (b) our characteristics, talents, and acquired skills and education; and (c) what roles (e.g., daughter, wife, employee) we have now or expect to have in the future and how we are going to behave in these roles. Consider how the Young Women theme (see page 53) recited every Sunday by young women is designed to help them understand their divine identity in the past ("We are daughters of our Heavenly Father"), how this divine identity should influence their present behavior ("stand as witnesses of God"), and what they should expect for the future based on their present behavior and divine identity ("enjoy the blessings of exaltation"). The theme also assists young women in understanding the importance of certain characteristics and experiences (faith, knowledge, good works), while also identifying the roles they have now (in their families) and in the future (receiver of the ordinances of the temple).

> We are daughters of our Heavenly Father, who loves us, and we love Him. We will "stand as witnesses of God at all times and in all things, and in all places" (Mosiah 18:9) as we strive to live the Young Women values, which are:
> Faith • Divine Nature • Individual Worth • Knowledge • Choice and Accountability • Good Works • Integrity • and Virtue
> We believe as we come to accept and act upon these values, we will be prepared to strengthen home and family, make and keep sacred covenants, receive the ordinances of the temple, and enjoy the blessings of exaltation.[45]

Significant life events, such as traumatic events, can prompt a profound reevaluation of our identity. We might question what we thought we knew, even things we thought we were most sure of, such as who we are. Consider how Amber felt when she lost sight of who she was and how she thought she lost her identity because pornography was part of her marriage:

> Through my years of marriage, I really lost sight of myself and who I was. I started isolating myself and stopped going out with friends. My self-worth was dropping. I had no self-esteem. I didn't feel pretty. He was continuously treating me like an object. There was absolutely no intimacy in our marriage. We never had deep conversations. We never talked about hopes or dreams or had any conversations of substance. He felt entitled to treat me however he wanted to in the bedroom and I allowed it. I was treated as a sex object—period.

Almost all of the women we interviewed told us how they had lost sight of who they were or had lost trust in themselves to make good decisions. While these processes may have been slightly different for each woman, we saw disturbing similarities in women's questioning of who they were and why they weren't enough for their husband once they discovered his pornography use. When women, who had previously felt that they were valued and treasured because of their unique attributes, capabilities, and appearance, learned that their spouse seemed to prefer virtual images with air-brushed physical perfection, it forced most women to ask why they weren't enough to satisfy their husband. Believing that they weren't enough or that their husband no longer had the same feelings toward them caused women to reconsider their identity—who they really were. Other women told us that their personalities had changed while living with pornography in their marriage, perhaps because they worried they weren't enough or the right person for their husband. For a few women, feeling like they weren't enough for their husbands led them to engage in sexual behavior or to participate in pornography with their husband when they felt uncomfortable in these situations.

The immediate disorienting shock of discovering a husband's pornography use causes some women to wonder how they missed the signs and to also experience intense feelings of shame at being deceived by someone so close to them. In some instances, the deception lasted for many years. Since they didn't question their husband before the disclosure, they started to doubt their previous perception of their life after learning about their husband's issues with pornography. Because confessions and full disclosures almost always revealed a secret or unknown but significant aspect of their husband's sexual activities, wives lost confidence in what their marriage or family was actually like in the past. They weren't sure what was real now that they understood how pornography was an unseen part of their marriage. Alice told us:

> I can't even look at photo albums, because it is too painful. I see those pictures and all I can think about is, *What was really going on in my life at that time?* It certainly wasn't what I thought. I just wondered, *Did you go to the strip club on this day? Was this a day you looked at pornography?*
>
> I really felt his love, and my love for him. I felt he was my soul mate, and I really did enjoy having sex with him. So, to think of those times now and realize that it was only one sided is so painful. I have to omit all of that because it wasn't what I thought it was. It is just like Alice in Wonderland. Nothing is real. It becomes whatever you want it to be. He will say that there were times when he was sober and that

he was connected to me, but he really can't remember when. He can't clarify any memories, so for me, they are all gone.

Being unsure of the past and what was real caused women to be disoriented about what they thought they knew about the past and present, and caused a lot of uncertainty about the future. In this chapter, we explore how these types of questions caused women to contemplate why they weren't enough for their husbands, who they really were, why they agreed to participate in sexual activities that made them uncomfortable, and if they could trust reality. Each of these questions is incredibly painful and uncomfortable for women to ask themselves.

"WHY AM I NOT ENOUGH?"

One of the most common responses to discovering that their husband was using pornography was for women to question why they were not enough for their husband. Some women started to question things about themselves that they might not have ever questioned before. Other women would wonder what they could have done to prevent the pornography problem. Too often the wife blamed herself for her husband's pornography use. This type of thinking is extremely damaging to a woman's sense of self and her self-worth, especially if her spouse continues to use pornography. Women often wondered why their husband turned to pornography instead of turning to her for physical or emotional intimacy. Melanie explained the difficulty of intellectually applying what she is learning about her husband's pornography use to what she emotionally feels about herself: "I really struggle to understand and believe when others say that a husband's pornography addiction has *nothing* to do with his spouse. No matter how many times I hear this I have a hard time accepting it."

After learning about the pornography, Dr. Skinner says a woman blames herself by thinking, *What if I would have taken a stronger stand against pornography?* or *I should have asked more thoroughly about pornography before we were married.*

> There are two scenarios. If her husband told her at the beginning of their relationship and pornography use hasn't stopped, she may think, *I wish I would have asked more questions. I wish I would have known more and taken this more seriously,* instead of thinking, *He's being open with me so that's great. I just wish I would have had more information.* The

second version is that she didn't know that he was involved, and now she is saying, *I must not have been smart enough. I didn't see the signs, something is wrong with me.*

A woman can go through a whole list of her deficits, "If I were skinnier, smarter, taller, better looking, had a different body, if I had taken care of myself, if I had eaten better, if I had given him more sex. . . ." They could go on and on. It becomes a list of, "If I had done this and if I had done that, then he wouldn't have gotten involved with pornography," incorrectly believing that her behavior could stop his behavior.

Why we make such assumptions about women's roles in their husband's life is troubling, but there may be some cultural explanations as to why this occurs. Young women are sometimes taught that young men will have impure thoughts if they dress immodestly (for example, "Don't dress immodestly or you'll become live pornography for men."). This message implies that a young woman, not a young man, is responsible for the young man's thoughts. Some of the women we interviewed felt strongly that this is a misguided way to teach young women and young men about modesty; specifically, teaching young women that they are responsible for a young man's thoughts. Another common cultural message is that, "Behind every good man is a good woman." So what is the converse of that? Behind every man with a pornography problem is a woman who also has serious problems?

In reality, a man who is starting to look at pornography or who has a pornography addiction is not reacting to his wife's appearance or the frequency of sex. Often men are addicted to pornography even before they meet their wives. Further, LDS beliefs in agency necessitate that men and women be responsible and held accountable for their own thoughts and behaviors.

Shirley was one of the women who really struggled with the concept that her husband's pornography addiction had nothing to do with her. After attending 12-step meetings, she was better able to avoid personalizing her husband's pornography use. She said:

> As I learn more and more about the nature of the disease, I take it less personally. I now feel like it is *not* an intimacy issue, but it is an addiction. In Sex Addicts Anonymous (SAA) and other 12-step programs you learn this. You learn that it is no longer about sex. Therefore, you take it less personally. It is no longer a reflection on you or your

self-worth. You start to realize that your worth is no longer based on how your husband feels toward you, but on how much Heavenly Father loves you. I am no longer defined by what my husband thinks about me or the choices he makes about using pornography. It has taken a while to get to this point, but this is where I am today. My worth comes from who I am as a daughter of God.

Some women, like Shirley, eventually learn to not take their husband's pornography use personally, but learning how to do this can be difficult. It is a process that takes time, and you must gain an increased understanding of the nature of addiction, and make a conscious effort to continually tell yourself that you are comfortable with who you are.

"WHO AM I?"

Many women we interviewed realized that their identity had changed because of their husband's pornography use. In Steffens and Means' research, one woman told them, "[My husband's addiction has] altered the way I see myself; it's affected my personality—I'm not free and fun like I used to be. I'm not even the same person anymore." [46]

Ashley, whose story will be shared at the end of this chapter, was married at age nineteen and found out about her husband's pornography use after thirteen months of marriage. She told us how her identity changed over time, without her even realizing it.

> Michael had this temper and would get angry, so I felt like I had to be this submissive, kind wife that could never speak her mind just so I didn't set him off. This was not at all like who I had been. There was one day in particular that we had gotten in an argument because he didn't want to be intimate with me. He told me that was the last day he had viewed pornography. I became this kind, soft-spoken wife who wanted to think I was still sassy and outspoken, but I really wasn't living my life that way. I wasn't that independent person anymore.

Likewise, Melanie explained how she went from being really confident to thinking she was an "idiot."

> Before we got married, I was really confident. I would always stick up for myself whenever he or anyone else challenged me. But after we were married and he continuously belittled me about different things, it definitely affected me. When he would treat me this way, I would just not talk or share my opinion. I would tell him that I was so sorry for

being such an idiot. I told him that all of the time. Now when I share my opinions I am able to realize when he is getting defensive and when he is doing things that are not okay. I have a right to discuss what I want to say, and even if he doesn't agree with it, he doesn't have a right to make me feel stupid.

Reclaiming one's identity is a process that occurs over time and involves considering who one was in the past, understanding how the present situation has altered one's sense of self, and deciding what one would like to be in the future. Acknowledging one's strengths and talents, including the strengths that have been gained by having pornography as part of a marriage, can also assist women in reclaiming one's sense of self.

"WHY DID I DO THAT?"

A few women felt that they had lost their ability to trust in themselves when they participated with their husband in using pornography or engaged in other uncomfortable sexual behaviors. It may be difficult to grasp why women would engage in such activities, especially if they knew the behavior was wrong. However, understanding that women wanted to please their husbands, that they worried they weren't enough for their husbands, or that they had lost their core identity might be possible explanations as to why some would do things they knew to be wrong. Eventually, though, women who had done such things examined their behavior, realized they didn't want to do these things, and eventually deeply regretted participating in such behaviors. Susan said, "I kind of suspected [he was using pornography] when he tried to draw me into the behavior. He would say to me, 'Well let's . . .' and I think in his mind he's thinking *If she participates, then it's not really a betrayal. I'm not really cheating.* So he tried to draw me into the activity by watching it with him. I think I did twice. Then I just went, 'Oh, heck no. This is not working for me.' I just felt like scum after." Amber said, "He started introducing things into our sexual relationship that I felt uncomfortable with. He would bring home sex toys that he had bought when he was alone at an adult store."

Jeanne, who went from being Relief Society president in her ward to pole dancer for her husband and his friends, explained,

> I thought, *Wait a second. If you really do adore me, if you really worship the ground that I walk on, if you really, really, really love me like*

you say that you do, how could you offer me up? I'm supposed to be your prized possession, something that you adore. We got sealed in the temple and that was special. I just started feeling really dirty. I didn't feel like I was supposed to feel. Not like how I was taught that you were supposed to feel.

This extreme example sadly illustrates how a woman not only loses her identity due to her husband's pornography use, but how her self-esteem can become so fragile that she feels the only way she can save her marriage is to participate in these type of activities. Jeanne shared how she eventually turned to drinking alcohol to numb her from the emotional and spiritual effects of her behavior. Jeanne has since ended her marriage and has found peace through repentance and volunteering in 12-step addiction programs.

"WHAT IS REAL?"

After discovering pornography had been part of their marriage, many women started to doubt their past perception of their marriage and who their husband really was. Alice told us it was a lot like Alice in Wonderland because things she thought she *knew* really weren't as they seemed. When Sarah's husband detailed his past pornography use, she wanted him to stop telling her the time frame because she felt it was hijacking her happy memories. Eventually, she came to terms with the fact that her emotions were real to her.

At one point during his detailing of everything that happened I realized that all of my memories of life with him had been hijacked. What was *real* about my life? He started telling me things like, "Remember that time you came down in the basement at my mom's house? I was looking at porn. When you went to visit your parents, I never looked that week, but I looked the morning you came home. I looked before I went to the airport." I wanted to say "Stop telling me the time frame" because I didn't know if the joy I'd felt throughout my marriage was real anymore. However, I had a strong impression that all of the happiness I experienced in our entire marriage was real. Everything was real. When I felt the confirmation from God to marry Hank that was real. When I married him in the temple, that was real; that was real joy. When I held my son for the first time and I watched Hank as a loving father that was all real. When he gave me priesthood blessings and he wasn't worthy, I still felt direction. It was all real for me. I was happy. I was just grateful that God allowed me to be happy when my husband was living his own personal hell. I was truly happy during that time.

For women who had no reason to suspect that their husband was using pornography, discovering the problem caused women to doubt their ability to know if there was a problem in the future. This is how Cynthia described it:

> After his disclosure, I felt like we were progressing in the right direction, but then I remembered that I thought things were going well before his disclosure. Truthfully at any moment my husband could walk out that door and never come back.

As women struggle to develop trust in what their husbands tell them, many learn that he has minimized, denied, deflected, or even offered fake confessions about his pornography use throughout their marriage. When women suspect a new incidence of pornography use or that something isn't quite right with their husband, they may confront him. Sometimes women feel like the Holy Ghost has told them their husband has been using. However, when women talk to their husband about their concerns, they are left wondering if his response is true, partly true, or completely false. This becomes a pattern of interaction between husbands and wives, a dance of sorts, around what is actually true about their husband's pornography use. This dance of deceit can happen over and over across many years. During our interview, Claire told us, "There has also been a lot of me not trusting myself because I feel that [my husband] has been lying, but he says that he has not." Alice also shared how this dance of deceit caused her to not trust herself.

> You just start wondering if you are crazy. I cannot pinpoint when I was paranoid and he was doing fine versus the Spirit was telling me versus it was my eating disorder thoughts. I not only didn't trust others, I didn't trust myself.

Ashley's story also illustrates many of the points in this chapter. Although Ashley had been married for only thirteen months, she still experienced the process of identity fracturing that can occur in the face of emotional abuse and traumatic experiences. Many times, she questioned why she wasn't enough for Michael, especially when he wasn't as interested in being as physically intimate as she was. As Ashley's story continues to progress, she is beginning to understand how Michael's past pornography use is tied to their lack of physical intimacy. At the time of our interview, Ashley had known about Michael's pornography use for only two weeks and was only just beginning to start to reassemble those fractured pieces and to reconstruct who she is.

ASHLEY'S STORY

Michael and I have been married a little over a year, about thirteen months. I just learned about his pornography problem two weeks ago, so everything is still very fresh to me. When we were first married, everything was fine. He was a strong priesthood holder. We both had callings in our ward, and I thought everything was great. And then things began to change.

He didn't really want to be intimate as often as I did, and I thought that was strange for a man his age. When he would come home, he would just go lie down and look at his phone. He never wanted to be with me. I was that pathetic wife who had cleaned the house and wanted to have dinner together, and he was always too tired or had a headache or wasn't feeling well. I would go into the room and try to cuddle up to him and he wouldn't want to. I would try to kiss him, and he would just turn away. Every day I would make sure the house was cleaner than the day before, that the meal I prepared was better than the day before, and that I was more attractive than the day before, but with him it seemed that nothing was ever good enough.

So many things started coming to mind as reasons why he didn't want to be intimate with me. I had gained weight since we had been married, and so I started thinking things like *Maybe it's because I'm not thin enough.* I had donated my hair, and so I thought *Maybe it is because my hair is not long enough.* I did wonder if he was looking at pornography, but I never asked.

And when he did want to be intimate, he was aggressive. He liked spanking, and I didn't like that at all. I would ask him not to, but he still did it. There were other times that he tried things we hadn't done before. At times, he was fierce with me; there was a lot of rolling; and he would try to pick me up. I was not comfortable with that. It seemed like we were in a pornographic movie. I felt like he was trying to re-enact something that he had seen before. There were things he would try and do that I would think no one would do this unless they had been viewing something inappropriate.

I was confused as to whether he cared about me or not, or whether he still wanted me as his wife. I always asked him if I wasn't the wife he was supposed to marry because he treated me that way. We argued a lot, and there was a dark feeling in our home. There were times I didn't even want to come home because I felt happier and more spiritual at work. I really didn't enjoy being around my husband anymore because it was too stressful. This really bothered me.

When I finally did ask him if he was looking at pornography, he really tried to avoid it and dance around it. He would say, "I am just stressed." He was short tempered too, but he always said it had to do with stress. It made me feel like I was giving him too much to stress about. We really had stopped being intimate. I started keeping track in a planner about the days that I was denied intimacy.

Over the next few months, I asked him so many times because I really felt like he was viewing it, but he would blow it off and even accuse me of being the crazy one. I felt crazy. I always felt that there was something going on, but he would always deny it. He would just be like, "Oh, it's just your emotions; you're being hormonal." I hate when boys use that against us. It always rubs me the wrong way.

The day he came clean we were arguing because I knew something was wrong but he kept denying it. I decided to listen to general conference. I recommended that he listen to it with me so we could be in a better position to talk. After listening he said, "You are right, there is something wrong. I have been viewing pornography. It started when I was seventeen years old." He told me he viewed it on his mission and since he'd been home.

I felt so alone and really didn't know what to do. I packed up his clothes and threw them out. I tore up all of our wedding pictures that were hanging up on the wall and cut him out of them. I wanted him to see that he was cut out of all them. That was kind of a funny moment for me. Who would have thought that this would happen at my age? I'm only twenty years old. I just never thought that at age twenty this would happen to me.

When I found out, I felt like it was my fault. Maybe I didn't dress myself up well enough, maybe I should have been more concerned with how I appeared, how I was performing in our household. I had been going to a lot doctors because I had been depressed. They had given me a diagnosis of depression, which was so weird because I had been such an optimistic person. I was put on different medications, which is how I gained most of this weight. What was so hard for me was that he saw there was something bringing me down and he never said anything about it. He never came clean, and he never thought that something he was doing was affecting me this way. He had so many chances to come clean and start this process earlier. It would not have been so damaging to our relationship.

Since his confession, I have definitely had flashbacks of him telling me. I thought he was disgusting, and I remember that night I went to a friend's family's house for a girl's night out, and then I came home, and I didn't really know what was going on. He had stayed up, and I had stayed out until 3 a.m. because I really didn't want to go home. He had been watching family videos and he was acting so sweet. I was completely disgusted by him. I didn't want to be in the same room as him. I didn't want him to touch me. I do feel guilt now because I do care about him, and I do love him, but it is still hard. I still sometimes get those feelings of disgust.

I get caught between the notion that I don't want to be his mother and his lover, his warden and his wife. I know that I need to set up boundaries and then it begins to feel more like I am his mother and it is really hard to do that. But I just feel like I have to restrict him from things. He has rules that I have set up. For instance, he can't be on the computer unless someone is with him. He can't get on the Internet on his phone. There are things he can't do on his phone.

I find myself constantly worrying about him. Is he viewing or coming across something inappropriate, something that will totally set him off? Last night I tried to call him and he didn't answer. Then the worry kicked in: "Oh, my gosh! He is viewing pornography again. He is looking at it right now and there is no way for me to know because I am not at home with him." So this is another time when I start to feel like his mom and not his wife. I am always worrying about him. It has become easier to just not feel because I don't know what is going on or what is going to happen. My mind is in a daze—I am in a daze. I'm still trying to cope with this.

I feel like he has had so many chances to be honest with me. Before we were married, I told him things about my past. He had many chances to be honest with me. There is a part of me that wonders why I am married to someone I can't trust and who isn't honest. I feel like I was honest in our whole relationship and he needs to reciprocate that. That isn't happening so I am very angry about it. He always believed that he could fix it on his own. He and his family always swept things under the carpet rather than deal with them, and they still do.

I used to think that he was the spiritual one, more so than I was. But he has lost his temple recommend and right now he can't give priesthood blessings. That is hard for me because I was raised without a priesthood holder in my home, and I wanted the priesthood in my home. I go to the temple by myself now, and I never wanted that. I feel very alone spiritually. I feel like he still has a chance of getting back spiritually, but it is going to be a hard road ahead for him I think.

I feel like we need a change of scenery and a change in our lives. When we are making big changes I feel like we are moving forward. We have decided to find a different home because our home for a whole year was just full of dark, bitter, and angry feelings. There was not a good spirit in our home, and I need another place that doesn't have those memories for me. We are also getting different wedding rings. I'm wearing my original ring right now, but when I look at this ring I don't feel like I really knew the man who proposed to me. I don't know if I will keep my original ring because I don't want to look back. The ring means a lot to me, but it has three cords or bands to represent the three cords that are not easily broken. They represent God, the wife, and the husband. Now looking at it, it was something that was supposed to be so religious and sacred but he was not living that way. My new ring will be finished in a couple of days. I really like healing stones, so I got moon stones in my new ring. Moon stones are supposed to help a couple in a quarrel. Our new rings will mean more as to how we are now, like a fresh start. We designed the rings to resemble tree bark and copper. This to him represents stronger roots.

Right now is not a good time to bring children into our lives, and I don't think we should bring children into our home until we are clear of this. I'm looking at five to ten years down the road. He needs to work on himself, and I need to work on myself, and two unhealthy parents are not good for an innocent child.

It is hard right now to see the future because it hasn't been very long. I really care about this man, and I really love him. If it was an ideal world and there wasn't temptation, there wasn't Satan or pornography, I would see myself with him getting each other through school, venturing out into the world, having children, and building a home together, getting old, serving missions, and having a marriage of honesty and openness, trust and faithfulness. But I really don't know what the future holds for us. We are still so young and still trying to figure things out. I don't know if he is going to be able to kick this addiction. And I don't know if I can ever trust him again. Pornography is just right there on his phone or computer. It is everywhere. At this point I don't really know how he can gain my trust again. That's where the biggest battle is for me.

I just want to run home to my mom and have her help me get through this, help me heal, and help me start over. We have a lot of life ahead of us, so starting over without each other wouldn't be that difficult, but then there is the fact that he could get help, he could get better, and we could have a wonderful life together. Then I think, *He could get better and then marry someone else, and then where does that leave me? I still love him.* I constantly go back and forth trying to do what's best for him and what's best for me. When I talk to my family and friends about this, many of them tell me that I need to be there supporting him through this, but I believe that I also have to take care of myself through this. I love him and I care about him. We have built a life together even though it's only been thirteen months. But then again, this relationship wasn't based on honesty and trust. So for me, it is so fresh. I am really torn. There is a part of me that feels it would almost be easier if he had cheated on me because, without a doubt, I would have left him.

The other day as I was praying, the thought came to me that choices have been his, that because of his choices we are having this trial. But I realized that some of the strongest women fight through this. You have to keep your head up and stay grateful and classy. That's my outlook right now.

I have discovered that I like to be alone. I like to ponder my life and the lessons I'm being taught. I don't mind hanging out by myself. Right now I just like to hear my thoughts. I like to hear what I have to say. I want to know what I think about things. When I get in a car I don't turn on the radio—That way I can listen to what I am thinking. It's fun talking to myself. I took my dog on a hike the other day and I really enjoyed getting to know myself again and what I want in life.

The biggest thing right now is that I am getting back to who I was. Life is like a hike, and I'm deciding if I want to keep taking that hike or if I'm going to give up. Whether I have someone next to me on the hike or not is going to be up to him. He is the one that has to make that decision.

LOSS OF SELF IN ASHLEY'S LIFE

Ashley's story, along with so many others, indicates how women suffer the loss of their identity and self-worth when pornography is present in their marriage. This loss at first goes almost unnoticed, but day after day of a lack of intimacy, being made to feel that they are never enough, and that somehow they are responsible for their husband's behavior eventually takes a toll on women's sense of self. As a result, many women like Ashley succumb to depression and isolation, and they worry if their spouse wants to be married at all or if he even cares about them. This becomes painfully confusing to women because they have heeded the counsel to become one with their husband, and by so doing their identity has become completely intertwined. In a healthy relationship, this intertwining ironically produces more independence for a husband and wife to fulfill their roles in marriage. However, when a pornography addiction is present, that same intertwining is based upon lies and deception, and instead of producing independence and self-worth, codependent behaviors ensue and a loss of identity results. All of a sudden, the person they once thought themselves to be no longer exists.

At this point, women find themselves in a precarious emotional state. They grieve over a past that never existed, and eventually must let go of their perceived idea of what the future would be. Women mourn as they bury their previous-held beliefs and feelings about their husband and marriage. It becomes difficult for women to project into the future since the past wasn't what they believed it to be. The present and future are full of pain and uncertainty. In this situation, women must realize the importance, as did Ashley, of relearning who they are, and rediscovering their self-worth.

In conclusion Dr. Skinner told us:

> I think that a woman's suffering begins with the fact that, "I am married, and I had this expectation, and now I am mourning the loss of what I thought I had." That goes hand in hand with all of the other questions, the fears, the worries, the trepidations, and the thoughts of, *What does this mean? Who is this person I'm married to?* In therapy, when we come to understand this and couples learn to work through this, they start to see each other in their suffering.

LOSS OF INTIMACY 4

Secrecy is the enemy of intimacy. Every healthy relationship is built on a foundation of honesty and trust.[47]

– Dave Willis

Intimacy, whether it is sexual, emotional, social, spiritual, or intellectual, is important to the health and success of any marriage. However, because of their husband's pornography use, most women told us that their marriages lacked most or all forms of intimacy, and that intimacy was difficult to develop and maintain. This lack of intimate connection left women feeling insignificant in what they believed should be their most important relationship.

Church leaders and professionals alike have addressed the lack of intimacy that is created when one uses pornography. Elder Dallin H. Oaks has said, "Pornography impairs one's ability to enjoy a normal emotional, romantic, and spiritual relationship with a person of the opposite sex,"[48] and Elder M. Russell Ballard has said that pornography "kills genuine, tender human relationships" and that it "fosters unrealistic expectations and delivers dangerous miseducation about healthy human intimacy."[49] William M. Struthers wrote, "Time spent with porn prevents the user from engaging in real relationships with real people who can better meet their needs."[50] Steffens and Means have said,

The porn addict has learned to substitute intimacy with a quick and easy fix instead of investing time and energy into doing the emotional and relational work true intimacy requires. The addiction itself blocks both a secure attachment bond and authentic intimacy.[51]

Sadly, Amber told us how there had never been intimacy in her marriage, yet she remains hopeful that one day, true and consistent intimacy can exist. Note how Amber intertwines her hope for intimacy with trust and honesty.

We never had intimacy. Ever! We would have sporadic spiritual intimacy, like going to the temple, but now that I think about that, he was never worthy. That makes me sick to my stomach. Also, his crazy-making tactics are still in force. This really impedes our intimacy on all levels. When I think about the future of our relationship, I picture open and honest communication. I picture a higher level of intimacy (on all levels) that was never there before. We never even had physical intimacy; it was just sex. I envision trust—being able to trust him again.

We asked Dr. Skinner what areas of intimacy are most affected when there is a pornography addiction in a relationship and why it impacted intimacy. He told us:

Every aspect of intimacy is influenced. When I talk about intimacy, I am not just referring to the physical or sexual aspects of intimacy. I am also referring to emotional intimacy, the sharing of emotion; verbal intimacy, the sharing of thoughts and ideas; and cognitive intimacy, those intellectual conversations. All of those types of intimacy are tweaked or altered [when pornography is present in the marriage]. The foundation of intimacy is trust and faith. If a person doesn't feel [emotionally, physically] safe within the relationship, then biologically it is almost impossible to connect, unless the person is over-riding his or her natural system to connect with you. There is a significant amount of research that shows that only when we feel safe do we become vulnerable and open up to other people. Stephen Porges's work, the polyvagal theory, describes the first thing we do when we are in a situation (for example, when we first enter a room): we automatically and subconsciously check for safety. So when we are in a relationship where we are trying to connect with each other, it is fundamental for each person to try to determine if they are emotionally safe. When this type of safety is not present, a person has to override their [biological] system in order to be intimate in any way.

SEXUAL INTIMACY

Sexual intimacy is a major area where women struggled in their marriages. Even thinking about being sexually intimate with their spouse often caused women to experience fear, confusion, and feelings of being unsafe, especially right after pornography use was first disclosed. When women did engage in sexual intimacy, they were sometimes left feeling degraded, used, unimportant, and disconnected. Sarah shared the pain and heartache she experienced upon realizing her and Hank's sexual encounters were often him just finishing an earlier pornographic fantasy. Other women shared how difficult it was to not compare their bodies to the perfect bodies they imagined in pornographic images. The thoughts and images contribute further to the emotional disconnect that is already occurring during sexual encounters. Furthermore, when women were pregnant, comparing their pregnant body to an imagined perfect body that might be seen in pornography was particularly distressing. One can only imagine myriad thoughts and feelings these expectant women experienced.

There were also times women knew their husbands had been looking at pornography because of how his behavior changed during sex. For example, husbands might spank or play rougher during foreplay, as Ashley told us in the last chapter. Women painfully recognized that this behavior had been influenced by pornography and were reminded that their husband viewed her as an object. Other times, husbands would introduce something new into their sexuality, which would immediately trigger women, causing them to wonder if men had learned this new sexual behavior from watching pornography. William M. Struthers summarized the dilemma inherent in sexuality when pornography is in the marriage.

> Pornography corrupts the intimacy that a man and woman can experience together because of the baggage it inherently brings with it. Men believe they should make love like a porn star to a woman who should look like a porn star. Rather than being who he is with the woman he is with, he measures his performance against the performers he has seen. (Porn stars often refer to themselves as "performers," suggesting the sexual encounter is not an emotionally real one.) He

evaluates the staged intimacy between two performers (not himself and his wife) against his sexual relations with his wife. He cannot be fully present; he is assessing his "performance." Intimacy in marriage is further corrupted by the man measuring the woman he is with (whom he should be focused on) against the woman on the screen. Pornography is the recording of sexual intimacy between two human beings, whether authentic or not. When it is consumed by another, it intrudes on how that person is able to be intimate with their partner.[52]

Reinforcing what Struthers has said, Alice told us,

His addiction has destroyed intimacy, because he is incapable of knowing what that even looks like. He has created pathways in his brain based on pornographic images. . . . He is learning to think differently about life. He is, for the first time, discovering what intimacy really means and what human connection is. . . . He is learning not to objectify me and other women and he is discovering that we are equal. I am not his toy, and I am not his little pet.

During the interviews, some women would say their husbands were addicted to "lust" rather than pornography. Others may feel that they are one in the same. Elder Jeffrey R. Holland has clarified, "If we stop chopping at the branches of this [pornography and infidelity] problem and strike more directly at the root of the tree, not surprisingly we find lust lurking furtively there."[53] Cynthia told us that she was struggling to figure out what lust was compared to love in her sexual relationship with Thomas.

I have been feeling that the only connection we have lately is sexual, so any kind of touch or anything like it makes me pull away. It just feels too much like lust lately. I feel like it starts out as lust and then turns into a desperate plea for reassurance from me, and I just can't give it. I thought I had explained myself to him in a way that was clear, but I guess I didn't. He took it as anytime we have sex I interpret it as lust and that makes him feel like a mindless animal that has needs that have to be met, and he questions his worth when things like that come up. So I just tried to clarify that I don't believe that our entire sex life is based on lust and the way we have sex is okay, but I just need to feel, beforehand, the reasons behind him wanting to have sex, because I often feel like a pile of conveniently located female organs. And that is so painful to feel like that.

Cynthia and other women want to know they are loved by their hus-
bands, but when pornography is present, the lines between love and lust
become clouded, particularly for the addict. Elder Holland continued his
comments on lust by comparing them to love, as is seen in Table 2. This
list may help couples who are struggling to understand the differences
between love and lust.

TABLE 2. LOVE COMPARED TO LUST
(ADAPTED FROM ELDER JEFFREY R. HOLLAND[54])

Love	Lust
Endures and has permanence	Changes quickly
Is shouted from the housetops	Is characterized by shame and stealth; is almost pathologically clandestine
Makes us reach out to God and others	Celebrates self-indulgence
Comes with open hands and open hearts	Comes with an open appetite

Table 3 (continued on page 72) contains descriptors of healthy sexu-
ality compared to porn-related sexuality. Notice the similarities between
this list and that of Elder Holland concerning the differences between
love and lust.

TABLE 3. HEALTHY SEXUALITY VS. PORN-RELATED SEXUALITY
(MODIFIED FROM MALTZ & MALTZ[55])

In Healthy Sexuality, Sex . . .	In Porn-Related Sexuality, Sex . . .
Is caring	Is using
Is authentic	Is deceitful
Enhances your identity	Compromises your identity
Increases emotional bonding	Increases emotional separateness
Enhances spiritual unity	Increases spiritual separateness
Is morally saturated	Is free of moral convention
Requires communication	Does not require communication
Is other-directed	Is selfish, self-directed
Involves all of the person	Is visual and genital

In Healthy Sexuality, Sex . . .	In Porn-Related Sexuality, Sex . . .
Naturally drives us toward intimacy	Unnaturally drives us toward compulsion
Nurtures the spouse	Hurts the partner
Is an expression of love	Is an expression of lust
Humanizes	Objectifies
Provides emotional, moral, psychological, and relational clarity	Produces emotional, moral, psychological, and relational confusion

In addition, Struthers has commented that pornography causes individuals to focus on the physiology of sexual sensations rather than on a deep emotional connection between a husband and wife.

> The experience of sexual intimacy is properly intended between a husband and wife in a maturing healthy relationship. When pornography is acted upon, sexual technique replaces sexual intimacy. In the absence of a meaningful, relational context, nearly all of the elements of truly meaningful sexual intimacy are absent. Pornography teaches its students to focus on the physiology of sexual sensations and not on the relationships for which those sensations are intended.[56]

Sarah recognized the absence of sexual intimacy in her marriage and lamented her plight when she said that she learned about sexuality from her porn-addicted husband. She then shared her difficulty in learning about sacred and healthy sexuality.

> You always talk about sexuality in Church about being this sacred thing, but in the media you see, it's just all about the passion and the lust and the mechanics. You can't get the emotion and spirituality in a video or in a magazine. I think one of the issues that culturally the Church needs to deal with, in my mind, [is the belief that] any kind of sex is okay after marriage. Porn is the opposite of healthy sexuality, and I think Hank was taught, and I definitely thought, that anything you do after you are married is okay and sacred, and it is not. That is lustful sex, whether you're married or not. If he's having sex with me in that way then he's acting out his addiction.
>
> I'd been praying about and I know Hank was praying about what sacred sexuality actually looked like. Who teaches you that? How do you learn that? One time we were having sex and neither of us were focusing on mechanics, and it was all about connecting emotionally.

I feel like that is something I'm powerless over. I need God there help-
ing. I need Hank in a place where that same sacred feeling can happen.
Now I feel like there's sacred sexuality and healthy sexuality. They're
both good in marriage but they're not always there. There was a differ-
ence between the healthy and the sacred, and the sacred doesn't happen
as often as the healthy.

Sadly, some men told their wives that sex was the only way to feel
close to them, or that sexual intimacy was the only type of intimacy with
which they were comfortable. Claire said, "I really think that he wants to
be close, but he just doesn't know how. A sexual relationship is the only
way he knows how to be close." Courtney told us,

> I felt so unimportant and sex was like the most important thing
> for him. Everything else in our relationship was total crap, but if we
> were having sex frequently, then he was like, "Eh, I could live with you
> I guess." And vice versa. Everything else in our relationship could be
> awesome, we were talking, we were connecting, we were whatever, and
> if we weren't having sex, he was like, "I'm really not happy. I don't feel
> like we're connecting." And I'm like, "Yes, we are connecting. We are
> sharing a life together and you know me and I know you." You know,
> for me this is connection. Because sex was huge to him, it so screwed
> me up. I felt so unimportant. I know he wants me to be happy with
> sex, I know he does. But I just felt so unimportant. I felt like who I was
> didn't matter at all to him. It was like he was masturbating with me. It
> was so degrading to think, *I am just a sperm receptacle for you. This has
> nothing to do with me and it could be anyone or no one and you would
> still be just as satisfied.* That was what it felt like to me. And it was just
> degrading and awful and horrible and I'm still scarred.

While Elder Holland's talk titled "Of Souls, Symbols, and
Sacraments" is focused on the problems created when physical intimacy
is not expressed within a marriage, some of his language is equally appli-
cable to problems in marriage where pornography is used.

> Can you see then the moral schizophrenia that comes from pre-
> tending we are one, sharing the *physical* symbols and *physical* intimacy
> of our union, but then fleeing, retreating . . . of what was meant to be
> a total obligation . . . ?
> You run the terrible risk of such spiritual, psychic damage that you
> may undermine both your physical intimacy *and* your wholehearted
> devotion to a truer . . . love.[57]

INTIMACY ANOREXIA

If one or both partners put up barriers, avoid, or withhold nurturing the relationship, intimacy anorexia can develop. Intimacy anorexia restricts the free flow of intimacy much the way food anorexia restricts the intake of food. A pornography addiction is a common cause of intimacy anorexia, especially for men. It is important to note, however, that the addict is not the only one prone to intimacy anorexia. Recent studies have shown that 39 percent of women whose husbands are porn addicts suffer from intimacy anorexia.[58] Because of the traumatic nature of the husband using pornography, women can develop intimacy anorexic tendencies too, and they begin withholding their love and attention from their husband in order to protect themselves from emotional pain or because they resent their husband. Sadly, this intimacy anorexia can also transfer to relationships with other family members and to friendships as well.

We asked Dr. Skinner about women who develop intimacy anorexia as a result of their husband's pornography addiction. He shared with us how it is our natural inclination to want to connect with people, especially our spouse. Women's fear undermines this natural inclination and is the underlying cause of intimacy anorexia. Women are afraid of what they need the most—intimacy. He offers some insight into how women can keep from developing intimacy anorexia.

> If women can't get that kind of intimacy from their spouse, they need to consider other types of social connections. It is our natural inclination to connect or bond with other people. We are born that way. So when women develop intimacy anorexia, they are keeping themselves from connecting with individuals or people who can help them heal. If a woman stays in that intimacy anorexic mode, her friends and family will no longer see the person they once knew. They will not see this fun-loving, upbeat, smiling, teasing, giggling, naturally-relaxed person. They will begin to see someone who isolates herself—someone who stops attending family functions or distances herself from others. This bubbly, fun-loving person tends to disappear.

The disappearance of women's normal type of connection with others and women withdrawing themselves from social situations also contribute to the feeling that women have lost themselves as was discussed in the previous chapter.

Dr. Janice Caudill, a licensed psychologist, has identified a series of questions for the spouse to ask herself to determine if there is intimacy anorexia in her marriage:

- Are you starved for affection in the relationship? Do you feel loved and appreciated, or ignored and deprived?
- Do you feel as if you are married but alone in this relationship?
- Do you feel locked out from his feelings or as if yours are unappreciated?
- Does he shift the blame to deny responsibility or avoid looking at his own issues?
- Has your spirituality and self-esteem been systematically chipped away at?
- Do you feel rejected, unwanted, or unattractive to your mate?
- Is he controlling about money?
- Does he clam up when you try to communicate about something important to you?
- Do you worry about upsetting him or feel like you "walk on eggshells" much of the time?[59]

Lack of intimacy and emotional deprivation can result in a sense of isolation that can leave both partners feeling that despite being married, one is alone in the marriage. This can be especially true for the spouse not using pornography. Some women we interviewed told us that due to the lack of intimacy, they did not feel like they were married. Instead, it felt more like they were roommates with their spouse. Claire said it felt like she was in a fake marriage.

> I feel like I have been in a fake marriage this whole time. You cannot have an eternal marriage based on that. When it comes to the law of chastity, it is a fake thing in my marriage right now. There are no boundaries with that, and there is no dedication to that. In the past I have been like, "What is the point? Why shouldn't I be finding someone that I can connect with that cares about me?" I know that my husband does, but he is so taken over by this addiction that he doesn't ever show it, and it gets really lonely. So there have been times that I have thought, *I am just going to find somebody else.*
>
> Spiritually, I can only think of one time that we studied our scriptures together. We have had couple's prayer probably only five times our entire marriage. He has told me that it is more of a private thing for

him, and that he just doesn't feel comfortable. What I have determined is that he is just not comfortable connecting. If we go to a stake conference or watch general conference together, we don't talk about the talks because it is too uncomfortable for him to connect like this.

One way Claire thought she and Jonathan could gain some emotional intimacy was by going out on dates. She sadly laments, however, that he has been unwilling to do this.

> Another thing is that throughout our whole marriage I have asked him to take me out on dates. I told him it didn't have to be anything fancy. It could be as simple as going to a movie or playing games, but it had to be something. This way I would know that he was at least thinking about me. I think that he has looked at the computer ladies for so many years that he no longer realizes that real women have needs. I have needs. A date night is not a big deal. I have even made lists for him of things that we can do that are really cheap. He still has never done it. Never. I will plan a date night. If he doesn't want to go, then I go by myself. I don't do it every week, but if I need it I will go out without him.

Ignoring the intimacy anorexia has long-term consequences for the relationship. The spouse is lonely, as Claire describes, and it deprives the partner the opportunity of being fully loved and of fully loving in return. The long-term consequences predispose each spouse to bitterness, resentment, the demise of the relationship, and ultimate marital dissolution. Another possibility is that the partner may look for another relationship where love and intimacy are present.

Being isolated is also problematic for our physical well-being. Some researchers contend that emotional isolation is a more dangerous physiological health risk than either cigarettes or high blood pressure; thus the individual impact of intimacy anorexia can be enormous. According to Doug Weiss, the spouse of an intimacy anorexic could develop depression, hopelessness, lowered self-esteem, and feelings of despair.[60] We saw each of these characteristics in the women we interviewed. Dr. Skinner suggested that one of the best ways women come out of intimacy anorexia is to develop social relationships with people whom they can trust.

> One of the ways that women come out of that is by developing relationships with people whom they can trust, with whom they can be vulnerable, open, and connected. Women take it one person at a time and have deep bonding communication with that person. We have

done retreats where women have really learned to trust each other and have bonded with each other in a group setting. Women will share their story, and all of a sudden they start to not feel so isolated and alone anymore because they are around women who understand them. This becomes the process of learning that not everyone is scary.

My research shows that women start to question who they can trust and who they can't. Learning that there are still trustworthy people who can be there for them is fundamental and crucial to healing and recovering. You have to have social bonding and connection to heal long-term. You cannot remain in isolation, fear, and a lack of safety while expecting to heal. You just can't do it; it does not work.

Sexual anorexia is a specific type of intimacy problem that impacts pornography addicts in their marriage. Dr. Caudill sees a lot of overlap between pornography addiction and sexual anorexia. She says that the irony is that the same person who is out of control with a pornography addiction may simultaneously go for weeks, months, or years placing little or no energy into nurturing a sexual relationship with his partner.[61] One problem of sexual anorexia is that men may avoid having sex with his partner or may have difficulty getting an erection. Amber told us, "I would walk in when he was showering and he would be masturbating. It then got to the point that he was viewing pornography and masturbating so often that he could no longer get an erection in bed with me. I would lie in bed crying."

Dr. Caudill suggests that if you are a partner of an intimacy anorexic, you have a right to set the standard for how you will be treated in your marital relationship. You have a right to expect respect from your husband; you have a right to establish your boundaries in the relationship, including those that have short-term relational consequences and those that are deal-breakers; and you have a right to enforce consequences if those boundaries are violated.

Courtney, who initially experienced a healthy intimate marriage, eventually found herself struggling with the lack of intimacy she felt with Randy, who had a pornography addiction. Her story is an example of how difficult it is for someone to be vulnerable enough with her partner while trying to reestablish any type of intimacy. Courtney's story also illustrates the hope and healing that a qualified therapist can provide for individuals and their marriage.

COURTNEY'S STORY

I married Randy when I was twenty-one years old. I was quite confident that I was the oldest unmarried person on the planet earth and certainly in Utah. I was so excited to marry him. We were both so in love and very happy. We had dated for what seemed like an eternity but was really only a year. We were just connected, we were always on the same page, and we were so ready to be married. I was thrilled for our happily ever after to finally begin, but I was also aware of Randy's upbringing. His biological father was very abusive, and I knew Randy experienced a lot of really horrifying things in his younger years. Randy's parents separated and his mother remarried. He was then raised by his mother and stepfather. From that point on they were a happy, "normal" Mormon family.

Because of Randy's past, I knew we had a lot of emotional work to do. However, I knew that he was very aware of his own feelings. We were always open with each other, so I knew that when we were married we would be able to work through whatever came our way, and it wouldn't be hard because we already knew how. I was confident in our abilities as a couple to work through whatever life handed us.

Randy is what I affectionately call a serial confessor. He never lied to me. He never kept any secrets. He never did any of that. Isn't that what everyone wants: truth in their marriage? I had this, but all of a sudden I didn't want it. Within the first two months of our marriage, Randy came to me and confessed that he had a problem with masturbating. I was shocked! He told me that this is how he had dealt with his emotions from the time he was young. Later, he confessed to me that he had recently been masturbating to a Victoria's Secret catalog. This was almost a year into our marriage. His serial confessions showed up six months later, then three months later, then two months, and then it was over and over and over again.

We had a very active sex life before the porn. I was very satisfied. It was just fun and easy and relaxed and we were very comfortable with each other from the beginning.

Over time I watched Randy's pornography use escalate. He never hid it from me, so I was there every step of the way as I watched him spiral out of control. He was now viewing it longer and more frequently. It was heartbreaking to watch. It was no longer just a bad habit. Three years went by before we realized that this might be an addiction. Up until then, he could go for three or four months without viewing it. When he did view it, he would go confess to the bishop.

I really couldn't understand why this was an issue in our marriage. We were happy in my mind, and we were having plenty of sex. So I was troubled a little by the thought of *Why am I not enough?* I was hurt because I felt like I had been cheated on or betrayed. I felt a little abandoned. Each time he would confess to the bishop and come home and say, "He said I'm fine," I felt crazy. I thought, *Should I not be offended by this? Should this not affect me?* I wondered if I was making a mountain out of a molehill.

Each time he looked at pornography, he would confess to me. There was a time when he was looking at porn and masturbating three times a week. He was confessing to me every other day. I became so numb and disconnected. I would think to myself, "Well, another day, another loss, and there's nothing I can do about all of this." This tore my heart apart again and again. I was so frustrated because we would have the same conversation every forty-eight hours. He hated himself for doing this. He didn't view pornography because it made him happy and fulfilled. It was a compulsion. He simply could not go without viewing it. I would tell him that he was breaking my heart and that he had made everything so hard. He was ruining our lives, and I couldn't believe how quickly he could forget the pain that he was causing me. The pain was always still so fresh from the last time and then I would have to feel it all over again two days later.

My husband is really a nice guy and I'm much more brass and harsh. In my eyes and in the eyes of my family, I married up. Randy is very gentle, sweet, and soft-spoken. I'm just not. Whenever we were around family, I would snap at him, and my whole family would look at me like, "You are so mean to him." Then they would say, "You should try to be nicer." That annoyed me even more because they had no idea what was really going on in our marriage. Nobody understood that it was me that was really hurting. I still didn't even know why I was hurting, so I couldn't really explain it to them even if I was willing to, which I wasn't.

As Randy's pornography use escalated, we started to see a therapist together. My attitude was, "I don't know what's wrong with you. You have an issue. I don't know why you're so messed up. I don't understand why this keeps happening. I don't understand why you can't just stop it." The therapist's attitude, however, mirrored the bishop's attitude after Randy confessed to him. He told us, "This is not that frequent. This is not that extreme. This is not that bad." At this point I started writing on an anonymous blog to vent my frustration. After I had been writing on it for about six months, I had a comment come in suggesting that Randy's pornography use was an addiction.

We started seeing a therapist who specializes in pornography addiction. He recommended that we start attending the Church's Addiction Recovery Program (ARP) and a Passage meeting (an addiction recovery support group). Randy didn't want to go, but the therapist told me that I still should attend. I attended those meetings for two and a half years.

By the time I started attending the Passage meetings, I was completely creeped out by Randy. I remember one meeting where a woman shared her experience of being at a restaurant and overhearing the conversation of the table of women next to her. They started talking about icky porn addicts. Everyone at the table was saying, "I don't understand how anybody could be so creepy. They are all creeps." As this woman shared this in our Passage meeting, she became very emotional and said, "Our husbands are not creeps." I was sitting straight across from her and I was thinking, *Yes, they are. This is a very icky thing they are doing.* I could still see that Randy was a good person, but he still creeped me out. My emotions had escalated into hating him. In my mind, there was clearly something fundamentally wrong with him. He was bad. This is how it all connected in my head once we identified it as an addiction. This was a very painful part of my life.

Now that it was an addiction and I realized that this was going to keep happening, it didn't blind-side me anymore when he would slip up. However, I would still be crushed by each confession. I still struggled to understand *why* this was even an issue. Clearly there was a hole in our relationship. There was something wrong with me. I felt it was obvious to both of us that if there was not something lacking in our relationship and if we could stay on course, then this would not keep happening. So that is when I decided that I would do whatever it took to not let him relapse. I dug in and went to work.

To ensure he wouldn't relapse, I babysat him. I filtered our computers. I was his loyal and devoted go-to person. If he was having a hard time, he would call me and we would talk through it. I would try to build him up and keep him from doing the shaming thing. I made him start attending Passage meetings. He went once a week. I put in so much effort to help him with his addiction. I also made sure he was alone as little as possible. I was trying to have a lot of sex with him so that he wouldn't get the need. I did all of these things truly believing that I was going to fix him. I tried so hard to be a better person so that he would love me more and so our relationship could be more whole. The reason why he continued to relapse was that he wasn't putting anything into his recovery. He had nothing to lose. He wasn't even trying and I was wearing myself ragged.

I remember leaving my house for the first time after I had come to an understanding of what it meant to be codependent. I was going to a baby shower. I decided that I needed to let him handle his own stuff, so I told him as I left, "I'm not going to be available. I'm going out with my friends. I'll see you when I get back in a few hours." As I was walking home after the shower, I realized that he hadn't called or texted me once. I had fully expected him to contact me saying, "Help me," or "I wish you were here," but it didn't happen. As I came home, I was elated! I felt awesome! I was alive. It was now all on him. He had tried everything he knew to stay sober while I was gone, but to no avail. He was so torn up about it. I was only gone for three hours, but he made it sound like an epic war. He had failed. He had done the things that he thought would get him through it and it hadn't worked. I was flying high because he was finally feeling the pain instead of me feeling it. He was so depressed and so upset with himself. He sat there heartbroken and sobbing like a child. I had no responsibility in any of this. I had made no efforts. It was so fantastic! This then led to an enormous detachment for me. This detachment wasn't necessarily all great, though.

During my detachment stage I felt like the less I was involved with Randy and his addiction, the better he would be, and that didn't turn out too well. I detached too fast, and soon we were living totally separate lives. But at the same time, I felt like it was the only thing I could do. It was too painful to be involved. I knew I wasn't enough for him. I knew I wasn't pretty enough, smart enough, or caring enough. I was too mean. I was too judgmental. I was not whole myself, and I had my own set of issues. I was so disappointed in him, in me, in our relationship, and it just hurt. I hurt. And I couldn't do anything about it.

I hated him. I could not believe that I was dumb enough to marry him. I could not believe that he wouldn't just pull it together and stop it. I was just so disgusted by him. I thought, *This was not what a healthy person would do.* I knew what real recovery looked like and knew he was not in it. I couldn't figure out why he wouldn't just get there or do what he was supposed to do. So when I did the whole detachment thing, I just couldn't be with him. It was too much for me. In the detachment phase, I felt like I wasn't going to live with him like that. He wasn't healthy enough to have a real relationship with me, he didn't like me, and I didn't like him.

You hear about women who spend days on the couch after learning of their husband's pornography addiction. I didn't experience any of that. I was raised in a family where you just get it done. I was taught that sometimes life is hard, but you act like an adult, "buck up," and do it anyway. So that was what I did. I went to work, I did other things, and I built my life without him because it was too painful to have him be part of it. It had become too painful to be close to him. But during this time, he would still tell me about his slip-ups. He would drop it on me as I was walking out the door or he would call me while I was at work. I was irritated. I would think to myself, *Why is this my responsibility? This is not my fault that you can't get it together.* I fully expected him to do the dig-deep thing, and just "grow up, buck up, and stop it." I was annoyed with and disappointed in him. I was mad that he wouldn't just "man up." I just didn't see why it had to be so hard.

At this point, we stayed married out of necessity. It felt more like we were roommates. He was in school full-time and working full-time, I was running a business out of my house, and we had two kids. I needed a co-parent, and I needed someone to help pay the bills. It was too expensive and too inconvenient to separate. Neither of us were happy. We had frequent conversations about our unhappiness. We both knew that we were in trauma, and we didn't want to make any decisions until we sat where we were for a while. We continued going to therapy, and we tried to sort everything out.

We spent three years totally uninvolved with each other, except to fight with each other, to judge each other, and to pick on each other. There was no sense of intimacy at all in our relationship. We just didn't connect. We didn't see each other. I didn't want to see him. I didn't want to see who he was inside, to feel his pain, and that kind of intimacy just wasn't even an option for me. I barely saw him because we were both so busy. Looking back at this, it is so sad, but at the time it was painful and disappointing. This was not how my life was supposed to be. Anniversaries, birthdays, or Christmases would come around and I would think, *What are we celebrating? We have nothing to celebrate. We have these two beautiful children who we both love more than anything but we have nothing really worth celebrating. We're hardly a family.* That was hard. That was a really hard, depressing time.

At one point, I decided I needed to make some changes, but this time I would work on my happiness. I started an adult program with a new therapist, Dr. M. After doing a few assessments with him, I realized how incredibly unhappy I was. I'm a pretty anxious person, so he worked on a lot of mindfulness with me and taught me skills to help ease my anxiety. Randy eventually started coming to therapy with me once again. Dr. M helped us work through our feelings of loss that we had experienced in our relationship, and we've been able to connect more because of this.

Prior to Dr. M, I was just confused and I felt like nobody understood what I was saying. I was hurt that nobody was listening to my concerns. I have realized that once somebody heard me, understood me, and sat with me in my pain, then I could sit with Randy in his pain. The truth is he's not an evil guy who is looking for ways to screw up my life. That's not who he is. He is torn and hurt, and he is experiencing his own hell. Now that I can see his pain because somebody saw mine, I can move forward in healing. Before that, I had just hit a wall. I couldn't move forward because I had so much anger and hurt, and I really had a lot of fear that we would never be okay again. And now that I feel like I've been heard, that my feelings have been validated, and my experiences have all been real, I am free to begin my journey of healing. I don't think you ever really finish healing—but you can certainly progress in healing.

Dr. M had us do an exercise where we listed and then ranked the things that were the most important to us. He had us determine which things we wanted as the center of our lives. I determined that I wanted my relationship with Randy to be the center of everything. I wanted to love my husband more than I loved anybody else or anything else. This was critical for me because I realized that this wasn't my reality. I was not spending any time with him. He was not my go-to person. Whether I was struggling or I was happy, he was the last to know about it. He might hear about it from somebody else, or he would read it on my blog. From this point on, I decided that when something happened, I had to tell him before I could tell anybody else. I couldn't blab it on Facebook, I couldn't blog about it, and I couldn't text my friends until I had talked about it with him. I really made an effort to do that and eventually he became my go-to person. He became my best friend and the person that I trusted. When my kids did something adorable or when I was scrubbing poop out of the carpet again, no matter what it was, he was the first person that I told. I consciously created that habit.

Because of this, our relationship shifted. Not only was he my go-to person, I became his. Our relationship became whole again. We were sharing happy and sad things. We were discussing issues about the kids together. Instead of calling my mom or my friends when I had questions about my children, I would now turn to him. We certainly didn't solve all our problems that way, but we were at least attempting to. We were sharing our feelings with one another and he became a safe place for me again. We started making progress. We were becoming more than just roommates.

I used to think that trust meant you believed the words that were coming out of a person's mouth and that the other person wasn't lying. That was really hard for me because I had, by that definition, a very trustworthy husband. He was honest. He didn't lie to me. He told me what has happened because it was a relief for him to not be the only one carrying it. But trust is more about emotional honesty and figuring out what's really going on and what the feelings underneath are. And it's about trusting him to be gentle with my feelings and him trusting me. He needed to be able to trust me when he shared with me, and to trust that I was not going to condemn, shame, or judge him. I needed to learn that I could share with him my weaknesses and faults, my failures and concerns, and all my worries. Before, I would have no sooner told him that I was worried or that I was wrong about something than fly to the moon, because somebody had to be right and it clearly wasn't him.

Now I'm learning to say, "This is what I just did with the kids and that might not have been right. I have no idea." Clearly I don't know what I'm doing any better than anybody else does, but I need to be able to trust him with that insecurity and say, "I don't know if I'm right," and feel like he's not going to judge me or rub it in my face later. That he can come to me and say, "Oh, I really screwed that one up with the kids. That is not what I should have done. I still don't know what I should have done, but that was definitely not it." And for him to be able to trust me in that way is huge. In the past it would have been, "Well, of course you shouldn't have done that, you idiot. Read a parenting article once in your life." To me, trust and honesty used to be about saying true words, but now trust and honesty is being comfortable with our emotions and our insecurities and daring to find out what they are and then to share them with somebody. This is an enormously vulnerable, terrifying thing to do, especially with someone who has betrayed you.

I think spiritual intimacy is being able to share how we feel about God with each other. Since we went to church together and believed the same things and were both raised LDS, I thought that was spiritual intimacy.

I thought that other people who married someone not of their faith were going to have problems with spiritual intimacy. But not us, because we were both LDS, did it all right, and got married in the temple. I don't think that's what spiritual intimacy is anymore. I don't think it's about believing the same things. I think it's that ability to share my doubts or my concerns. If I don't have a strong testimony right now, can I share my doubts with Randy? To me that's spiritual intimacy.

When I lost spiritual and emotional intimacy with Randy, it was difficult to have physical intimacy. I feel like physical intimacy is more than sex—but that ability to be touched, to be physically touched and to be emotionally touched. It's that ability to bare your soul with somebody and to let them see your hopes and dreams and fears and worries and inadequacies without being defensive or afraid of what they'll think or do.

Randy has always been very physically affectionate to me. We would be somewhere and I would think, *Do not touch me that way in the grocery store.* It would stress me out. It would trigger all of that anxiety of sex being the most important thing to him. I would think, *Where is this coming from? Why are you turned on in the grocery store? Did you see somebody hot walk by? Have you been looking at the magazines at the checkout? Where is this coming from?* And I was terrified that it had nothing to do with me.

There were times when we were being intimate or fooling around or whatever, and he would touch me or look at me and I would think, *Oh my gosh! He's in porn land.* That would always send me off into that crazy anxiety spiral. Or he would say something while we were having sex like, "I love you," or "You're so beautiful," or whatever. I would say, "That is bull. Don't lie to me. That is just not true. There is no way you're thinking that." Because he had never lied to me before, it would trigger me into all of these other horror stories that I'd heard about these women who had been lied to for so long. I would think, *You're lying, and you've never done that before.*

The expectation of sex for me is totally crippling. I just feel like I'm performing. He brought porn into our sex life. Sometimes I would think when we were having sex, *Where did he learn that? Did he get that off of a video? How am I comparing? I know I'm not comparing because these porn people are like unattainably gorgeous and perfect and porn-y. I'm not. I'm not doing what they're doing or I'm not looking the way they look.* I would say to therapists and friends, "The porn is in our sex life, even if he's not thinking about it." Even if he can be fully present with me, I am thinking,

What else have you done? Why are you even turned on today? What have you been looking at? What have you seen in your whole life? Those images are running through my head even if they're not running through his. It was so damaging—so, so, so damaging—to our sex life.

I had to get to where I could say when we're having sex, "This is really hard for me because of x, y, or z. Right now I feel unimportant to *you*." And being able to look him in the eye and say "I feel unimportant to *you*" was huge. And it changed. That for me was what was healing for our physical intimacy.

I live in a whole different world now. I see everything through a different lens, but like I said, it's very recent for me to be able to fall back in love with my husband. I don't know that we're completely there yet. We're working on it. I know it will come eventually.

In my group therapy for people whose spouses are struggling with porn addiction, I was amazed at how suddenly I could see the good in their husbands when I heard the women talk. I could see the good in other people's husbands before I could see it in my own. I think partly this was because they saw their own husbands differently. It was crucial for me to see somebody else handle this in a way that was different from the way I was handling it. I had made all these friends who were from hugely different walks of life and at different places in their husband's addiction. My friends were in such different places in their journey: some friends were divorced, some were still married, some were working on living with pornography in their marriages, and some were just living in their marriages while not working on the pornography problem. But I suddenly saw all these women who somehow still loved their husbands. They somehow still felt like their relationships were okay.

It has taken a lot of therapy for me to get to where I am today—a lot of therapy. Now I see my husband as a man who has a million outstanding qualities and one super bad habit. I used to think that there was something fundamentally wrong, creepy, and just really icky about him. I can see it differently now. This is just a damaged piece of his life that, while not repaired yet, will eventually be okay. It is much easier now to see the good in him and all the good things he does. He has had these life experiences that have left him a little damaged, a little broken. But I have tremendous faith that he can be healed.

I know that someday we are going to be awesome. We're still very much in the thick of his addiction. This puts me in a really weird place to be when I speak to other couples about living with pornography in their marriage, or when I post blogs or make comments on Facebook, because a lot of the people who are involved or listening have already arrived at a state of recovery. But I know that Randy and I have such amazing potential. We are going to be cool, because we really are a good fit for each other. We balance each other out and keep each other grounded. He makes up what I lack, and I make up what he lacks. We are a really, really great team when we're both in a good place.

COURTNEY'S STORY AND INTIMACY PROBLEMS

Courtney's story illustrates the changes in intimacy that can take place in marriage when masturbation and pornography are introduced. Pornography's parasitic effects eventually render the marriage void of any semblance of intimacy. Marriages that once enjoyed the deep satisfaction of intimate exchange become nothing but an empty shell in which partners live detached lives, acting as mere roommates instead of equally-yoked partners. Wives with financial limitations similar to Courtney's may only function in survival mode because they cannot afford to separate and they need their husband to continue his co-parenting responsibilities. From Courtney's story, however, we learn that there is hope in the restoration of intimacy when both partners are committed to making it happen. Courtney did her part by seeking professional counseling for both the betrayal trauma and intimacy problems in her marriage. She implemented the counsel she received to put Randy first in her life. When the relationship with a spouse is paramount and commitment to intimacy has been restored, all forms of intimacy in your marriage will not only begin to develop but eventually flourish. Once steps can be taken to repair the breech in intimacy and trust that pornography has created, the total union of a married couple can be realized. Elder Holland has emphasized the importance of a total union of everything in a marriage.

> Human intimacy is reserved for a married couple because it is the ultimate symbol of total union, a totality and a union ordained and defined by God. From the Garden of Eden onward, marriage was intended to mean the complete merger of a man and a woman—their hearts, hopes, lives, love, family, future, *everything*.[62]

5 LOSS OF SPIRITUAL GROUNDING

There are times when we have to step into the darkness in faith, confident that God will place solid ground beneath our feet once we do.

– Dieter F. Uchtdorf [63]

In addition to feeling like they have lost themselves and the intimacy in their marriage, many women also experience spiritual pain and confusion as they attempt to reconcile their beliefs about marriage and the sacredness of the home with the knowledge that their husband is using pornography. As the spiritual pain continues, it may transform into a trial of faith. Women told us how discovering that pornography was part of their marriage caused them to re-examine their relationship with Heavenly Father. Some told us they were initially angry with Him and questioned why this had happened to them. Other women began to question their ability to receive revelation or inspiration from the Holy Ghost. Some experiences were spiritually painful for women—including their interactions with local priesthood leaders, the concept of a "worthy" priesthood holder, temple attendance, and sometimes even church attendance—because these were reminders of the disconnect between what they thought they had in their marriage and the reality of their situation. It often took years to process and find peace after the loss of their spiritual grounding.

SPIRITUAL PAIN AND CONFUSION

One of the sources of women's pain came from their deeply held religious beliefs about the sacredness of the marriage relationship, the importance of an eternal marriage, and the seriousness of sexual sin. These are all beliefs that make living with pornography painful and incongruent with core religious values, which is why a violation like this can feel like such a betrayal for women. Some women told us that they had dressed and acted modestly to ensure high standards in their marriage and felt cheated that they were not blessed with a husband who didn't use pornography. Women felt violated when pornography was viewed in the home, particularly if children were around. Some felt cheated out of their chance for eternal life or the promises that come from an eternal marriage.

As Latter-day Saints, we try to make our homes a sacred place, similar in sacredness to the temple. Frequently women consider it one of their responsibilities to create a sacred, Spirit-filled home. Many of the women we interviewed pleaded with their husbands to not bring pornography into their home. If husbands were not going to stop looking at pornography, women asked them to not view it at home. Women felt violated when pornography was viewed in their home because the pornography encroached upon a sacred space that they had created. Steffens and Means emphasized the importance of feeling safe in your own home:

> Nowhere is your need for safety more profound than within the walls of your own home. And nowhere does safety present such complications; after all, you share your life and space with your spouse and your need to feel safe within that protective space is *essential*. So regaining your sense of safety at home must become one of your highest priorities.[64]

In chapter 1, Sarah told us how it brought out the "mother bear" in her when Hank looked at pornography and then masturbated with their toddler in the room. Courtney similarly worried about her children when Randy used pornography in the home.

> My husband's porn use was always at home, so I felt like that was another part of that feeling of betrayal, like "I'm trying to create a happy, Spirit-filled environment here, and you're chasing that out. You're throwing off my groove and I don't appreciate it. I'm working really hard to do the things that will invite the Spirit into our home and

it's just not possible while you're doing this here." So that was another huge piece of that betrayal and worry. I still worry so much about my kids.

Cynthia also pointed to problems with a child that she believed originated from her husband's pornography use and the tension it caused in their home. One of her sons was suffering from severe nightmares and had problems falling asleep. After her husband came forward with his pornography use, she said:

> I just realized the other day that my son hasn't had a nightmare in months. I really do believe that his nightmares were related to my husband's pornography use and the extra tension it brought into our family. There is so much more peace and calmness and less darkness in our home.

Some women also worry that their husband's pornography use will influence their children, especially their teenage sons, to use pornography. Liz said sorrowfully that her husband's pornography use seemed to influence her sons to look at pornography.

> We had three teenage sons. At different times they admitted that pornography was a problem for them. That is when I had a really hard time, because I felt like somehow my husband had brought it into our home and now my boys had to fight the fight.

After learning about their husband's habitual pornography use, many women have wondered about their own chances for exaltation and eternal life. The Doctrine and Covenants teaches that "in order to obtain [exaltation], a man [and a woman] must enter into this order of the priesthood [meaning the new and everlasting covenant of marriage]" (D&C 131:2). Elder F. Burton Howard taught, "To those who keep the covenant of marriage, God promises the fulness of His glory, eternal lives, eternal increase, exaltation in the celestial kingdom, and a fulness of joy."[65] The women we interviewed who were married in the temple began to wonder what that meant for them in the new and everlasting covenant of marriage if their husbands frequently used pornography.

Courtney shared how painful it was to consider that the husband she thought was her "ticket to heaven" might not be the ticket for which she was hoping.

I had made enough mistakes in my life that I knew I was not going to heaven. I had not earned my way to heaven. And so I married him and he was going to be my ride. He was a really fantastic guy who did all the right things, and he was going to drive my car to heaven, and I was hitched to his star. Then I found out about his pornography problem and that he wasn't going to heaven either, that we were both damned for eternity. I felt totally betrayed. And now I see that was not fair to put that on him. Now I see how incredibly unhealthy it was. Now I see that neither one of us are going to heaven at all without God. Now I can see all of that, but at the time I felt like, "I hung all of my hopes and dreams on you. I put everything in. All my eggs are in this basket. I worked my whole life for *this* relationship, which in the Church and in my life is the most important relationship I will ever have. You screwed it up. It will never be the same as it was. Because the scars are still there, because our wings are now clipped, and we'll never reach the heights that we could have before." Because of all of those other messages that I held on to growing up, I was totally betrayed. This betrayal was so bitter because it encompassed everything—this was our eternity. I would remind him of this every time he slipped up. It became somewhat of a parting line as I tried to distance myself from him. I would say, "You took my eternal family and screwed it up and now I don't have a shot."

The uncertainty about one's own exaltation, eternal life, and fullness of joy can cause profound concerns and feelings of uncertainty about one's eternal future in addition to the feelings of uncertainty in this life. Cynthia, whose husband had a short affair, told us,

I really don't know where he stands before God, and I don't know what that means for my eternal welfare. I have made covenants, and I haven't broken any of them, and I am hoping that this is enough of a guarantee that I won't be left out. I also have hope that both of us will not be left out. I have hope that if he goes through the repentance process that it really will be valid despite the covenants he once broke.

LOSING FAITH IN GOD

When learning about their husband's pornography addiction, many of the women began questioning their belief in and understanding of God and His purposes. Often it was women's emotions (e.g., anger, distress) about having pornography in their marriage that triggered their questions about God. Alice was angry with Heavenly Father because of the flaws she perceived in men, who were created by Him.

> I was so mad at Heavenly Father, I was so mad. I just thought that He had totally rigged this thing. Here these men are and they have these hormones. Is this the plan? Is this how it is supposed to be? Men are so selfish, and He made them selfish.

Some women began to question their beliefs about God and His purposes for them in mortality. Courtney told us how she had to revisit her beliefs about God and how He worked in her life.

> As the reality of Randy's addiction set in, I questioned God a lot. I had prayed about marrying Randy, and God said I could. *Do I not know how to receive revelation? Was He lying to me?* During this time, I also had all of these other messed up ideas about God, like He's up there watching me and telling me, "Go ahead, marry him; let's see what happens. Just go ahead and try it." That is so messed up, but that was my idea of God. I truly thought that was how He was, and I was mad. I was always thinking, *I did everything I was supposed to do. I did everything right and it got me nowhere, so why should I try to do things right? Why should I even try to please God?*

Other women, such as Liz, told us that at times they felt especially close to Heavenly Father through scripture study and prayer. At other times, however, their emotions caused them to feel distant from everything, including Heavenly Father.

> My feelings about Heavenly Father are cyclical for me. There were periods when I couldn't do it on my own, so I poured my heart out in prayer for hours and hours daily to my Heavenly Father. I read scriptures and general conference talks constantly, and I felt really close to Him, and my spirit soared. While attending my 12-step group, my spirituality was up. Yet at other times, I was so angry. I pulled away from everything: my family, church, myself. I was just an empty shell.

Alice blamed God and would not let Him be close to her. Over time, however, her thinking shifted to a belief that He was there for her when she needed Him most. Eventually, Alice told us that she learned she could only trust in God because He would be the only one that would not disappoint her.

My Heavenly Father has always been there for me, but there were very real times throughout this process and my healing when I refused to let Him anywhere near me. I was hurt and I blamed Him. I was scared and didn't want to trust Him, so I would push Him away. I felt betrayed by Him because I was that girl, the one that did all the things I was supposed to, and this is how He repaid me? So I pushed Him away. But then I would need Him. I didn't want to, but I was so broken in the moment that I put my guard down, and He was there. I am still healing from betrayal trauma, but my Heavenly Father plays an active role in my healing because He never withholds His love from me. To Him I am worthy, I am valuable, and I am enough. So I cling to that when everything else makes me feel like I am not.

I have learned that you can only put your trust in God. You cannot put your trust in the arm of flesh. That pretty much says that you will be disappointed by your children and your spouse. I have learned that I have to trust the Lord.

Trusting in the Lord can be very difficult for women while coping with a husband's pornography addiction because of the many opportunities there are for spiritual fracturing to take place. When this fracturing does occur, Dr. Skinner feels that its origin may be when women are asking Heavenly Father if he approves of them marrying their husband.

If women are praying if they should marry this person and they get the feeling that, "This is a good idea or this is okay," and later they come to find out that he has a pornography problem, the women may think, *Whoa, I was getting my prayers answered and he was using pornography. He was hiding this, yet I received the revelation that I was supposed to marry him. Why would God do that to me?* Women begin to wonder if they can trust God.

One of the things that we as a society need to understand is that we put our trust in others; we trust that they will be reliable, not let us down, and keep their commitments. So when their commitment is broken or trust has been breached, we begin to see people that we thought were safe are not. I always go back to the safety of the relationship. Women ask themselves, "Is this person safe? Is this relationship predictable? Is it reliable?" It becomes a spiritual problem because they have put their trust in this person and that person broke their trust. Women may start to question, "Will God do the same to me? Why didn't God warn me? Why didn't God tell me? Why didn't He prevent this?" So now women are having this incredible spiritual battle thinking, *Why didn't You protect me? Why didn't I know this? Why didn't you give me inspiration?* And now they are questioning their own spirituality and their own ability to receive revelation, which is connected to God.

LOSING TRUST IN ONE'S ABILITY TO FEEL THE HOLY GHOST

Perhaps it is easy to see how someone who has believed that their spouse was worthy and making righteous choices (and perhaps *was* doing many wonderful things) would have their confidence shaken in their ability to discern the truth when they learned their spouse was concealing a pornography habit and regularly lying about it. The wives we spoke to, like many LDS women, had understood that they could receive guidance, counsel, and inspiration from heaven. Many of them had felt (to varying degrees) some measure of heaven's blessing on their marriage and had thought they had received spiritual confirmation and peace about their relationship. Now, in the light of new revelations regarding the depth of the lies, betrayals, and hidden sins, what should they make of such spiritual confirmations? If they could have been deceived by their spouse and for so long, perhaps nothing was what they thought it was; perhaps they had also fooled themselves when it came to other important, deep connections. Alice shared how she felt she had lost trust in her ability to recognize the Holy Ghost:

> I believe that the Holy Ghost does tell us the truth of all things, but once I realized that I had believed lies for years, I started wondering if something was wrong with me. I mean, how could I not have known what my husband was doing? What he was keeping from me? My conclusion was that I must be unable to recognize the Holy Ghost. So the Holy Ghost is a hard concept for me. I find that I think I feel the Holy Ghost, but then, because of my self-doubt and lack of confidence in my ability to recognize His whisperings, I talk myself out of something, or blame it on trauma or paranoia. My relationship with the Holy Ghost has been adversely affected by pornography in my marriage.

QUESTIONING ECCLESIASTICAL LEADERS

When women learned about their husbands' pornography problems, they usually told their husband to go talk to the bishop. However, many of the husbands had been going to see the bishop since they were young men in an attempt to stay away from pornography. One common type of advice priesthood leaders had given them was to read their scriptures more often and pray more diligently. During the interviews, a couple of women told us that they were so shocked to learn of their husband's pornography problem because he was the "spiritual" one in the marriage. Women defined the "spiritual" one as the one who consistently read the scriptures, prayed, and led their family in these practices. It may very well be that men who struggle with pornography for many years develop these habits because they sincerely want to overcome pornography and they have faith in following their priesthood leaders' guidance.

Over time, however, some women became very frustrated with the guidance priesthood leaders gave to their husbands. One problem was related to defining the problem as an addiction—for example, when bishops told the husband that he did not have a pornography addiction when others felt the label was obvious. A qualified mental health professional is the most appropriate person to diagnosis a pornography addiction. Courtney illustrates a typical conversation that ensued when her husband disclosed his pornography use:

> Each time he confessed I would tell him, "Okay, well, go talk to the bishop and then we'll be done and we can move on." For some reason it was so clear in my mind that all he needed to do was go and confess to the bishop, and then it would never happen again. We would be done with it. That was a ridiculous notion, but that's really what I thought. The bishop would tell him, "This really isn't that bad; it's not like you're addicted." From a bishop's perspective, I could see why he might say that, but it was not helpful at all. I felt completely invalidated by it because Randy's pornography use was really hurting my feelings. To me this was bad, and I didn't want to accept it as part of my life. I wanted this fixed somehow.
>
> I was hurt because I felt like I had been cheated on or betrayed. I felt a little abandoned. Each time he would confess to the bishop and come home and say, "He said I'm fine," I felt crazy. I thought, *Should I not be offended by this? Should this not affect me?* I wondered if I was making a mountain out of a molehill.

Many women realized that the addiction was a spiritual problem as well as an illness. While wives felt it was vital for their husbands to rely on the Atonement, pray fervently, and regularly read scriptures, they acknowledged that other types of help were needed as well. William M. Struthers said, "Using spiritual and psychological language to describe the tenacious grip of sexually destructive patterns is helpful. But calls to pray harder, move the computer to the living room, and get plugged into an accountability group only go so far. They come across as hollow."[66] Shirley's comments illustrate this point:

> I just strongly believe that our priesthood leaders need more knowledge, understanding, and training. Pornography addiction is a disease. But in the Church, we treat it only as a moral issue. It doesn't matter how much you infuse yourself with religion, scriptures, and callings, because those things really don't help you overcome this. This is a disease. The answer is not just a spiritual one. Prayer and scripture study are important, but they are only part of the equation. If you have cancer, you need chemotherapy. The same is true for healing a pornography addiction. You need a targeted course for your body to heal. This is an emotional and spiritual disease that requires targeted, specific help.

Alice, who spent time with other women whose husbands had pornography addictions, said that her friends viewed the priesthood as a cult of enablers. Shirley felt that priesthood leaders tended to use rescuing and enabling behavior that would allow the addict to continue in the pornography addiction rather than hold him responsible for his behavior. These leaders often failed to add an element of justice to their counsel in order to provide an opportunity for true repentance and healing. Sometimes the focus on mercy was difficult for women to understand. It is comforting to know that God is perfect in His mercy and in His justice. President Kimball said, "There are many people who seem to rely solely on the Lord's mercy rather than on accomplishing their own repentance. . . . The Lord may temper justice with mercy, but he will never supplant it. Mercy can never replace justice. God is *merciful,* but he is also *just.*"[67]

Additionally, these women sometimes received instructions from their priesthood leaders to change something about themselves, which exacerbated their feelings that if only they were different, their husband would not have a pornography problem. Another unfortunate outcome of leaders telling women that they needed to change was that some women stopped trusting their priesthood leaders as a source of spiritual guidance.

Liz explained,

> The thing that really hurt me the most at this time was a second church leader telling me I needed to be a better wife, spend more time connecting to my husband, and supporting him. He said if I did this, things would get better, and that I needed to spend more energy and time strengthening our marriage. I felt like I was being blamed all over again for the addiction and that this was all my fault. I was told that I didn't need personal counseling but just needed to work harder on my marriage and things would be fine. At that point I quit going to Church leaders for help or support. I just decided there wasn't anyone who knew how I felt or what I truly needed, and so I was just going to deal with this on my own.

Other women recognized that their husbands could minimize or outright lie to the bishop just as he had lied to them, their wives. Steffens and Means said that an appropriate question to ask clergy (i.e., priesthood leaders) is, "Do you know and understand sex [pornography] addiction well enough to realize the addict will probably lie to you, too?"[68]

Women also struggled with inconsistency in priesthood leaders' handling of their husband's pornography use. Of all the women we interviewed, Claire, whose own father was in a stake presidency, was probably the most vocal about the difficulty she had experienced in the past with priesthood leaders and how that had impacted her.

> We have been to ten different bishops trying to get help, as well as three different stake presidents or stake presidency members. I really felt like this was the only way I was going to get any help, but I felt like I couldn't get anyone to take me seriously or to follow through. A couple of months ago, I really went downhill. I didn't want to go to Church anymore because I was so frustrated. The only thing the bishops or stake presidents would say to me was to be more patient and to have hope. I thought, *What should I have hope in? Hope in an addict? Now that is a great thing to have hope in.* When my stake president tells me that divorce is not the answer, I just want to tell him that he has no idea what I have suffered because of this.
>
> Then we moved into this new house. I met a couple that I really liked, so I opened up to them. I asked him to give me a blessing. They also told me that I needed to go and talk to the stake president. I am so glad I did. This stake president said that we will work with him and that we do not put up with this in our stake. That was the first time I

ever started to feel any hope. My dad is in a stake presidency, and they don't put up with it in their stake either. This has been the only other stake that I have heard that. My husband met with our new bishop and he said the same things that had been said before, "You are going to be okay. You can overcome this addiction." I thought, *This is a bunch of bull.*

I then wrote a letter to the stake president and expressed my concerns. I told him that we are counseled to stay with our marriages, yet you offer no help in how to deal with these issues. Two Sundays ago, he called me and my husband in to meet with him. He told my husband that he is either going to be on probation or disfellowshipped from the Church because of this addiction. I have never had anyone get that close to anything like this. The stake president said that he was sorry that we hadn't had a chance in the past to get help with this, but that we are going to proceed in this direction so that we can help you, and by applying the Atonement we will be able to get through this. I have felt hopeless for ten years, but here we are now with a plan, a direction. The Church has always said that when there are problems, go to your priesthood leaders, but nothing has ever happened until now. I think my husband is feeling a little bit of hope too.

My dad told me that these are imperfect men, and that this addiction even after all these years is still misunderstood and that we don't talk about it like we should. I have worked really hard to maintain that attitude that they are really doing all that they can. But I have been told that I need to give my husband more sex; I have been told that I am being too hard on him; I have been told that there is nothing they can do, and that they don't know what they can do. I think that is a really big part of the problem. They simply do not know what they can do.

Women needed help and assistance of their own to deal with their husband's pornography problem, and they became upset when priesthood leaders seemed unable to see their need. Some felt that it would be better for bishops to say they do not know what to do rather than give harmful advice to them or their husbands. In Liz's case, her bishop told her she did not need personal counseling. This was frustrating for her because she felt like she did need help, especially with her depression. Alice was similarly irritated with the focus on men's needs while it seemed to her that women's needs were not considered.

Women really are neglected in situations like this. It is all about the addict. They make sure they visit with the addict once a week.

They make sure that they get them into therapy. We need to make sure that the addict feels supported and loved. In the meantime, the wife is wondering, *What just happened? So I need to support the man that just ripped my heart out and I need to make sure that I am gentle with him and that I don't upset him while he is going through this? Excuse me?* I don't agree with that. I've also been a little bit sad with my new bishop because I told him that even though Shawn and I don't go around and openly talk about this, I am more than willing to help any wife that is experiencing this. I am happy to help her navigate through this process and help her get the support she needs. In the past five years, no one has asked for my help and support, and I don't know if the bishop has even offered it.

While many women acknowledged the priesthood leader was doing the best he could, they expressed a concern over a lack of adequate training. In frustration, Minnie said, "Bishops are clueless. They have no idea, they don't know how to counsel this, and they don't know how to counsel a wife who is going through this."

Dr. Skinner told us that there has been a great deal of training for bishops in the Utah Valley, Utah, area, but there are still bishops that do not understand the woman's perspective. He notes that it is not only LDS bishops because there are other religious leaders across the United States who wonder how to deal with couples who are dealing with this problem. It is difficult to understand what betrayal trauma, caused by a husband's pornography addiction, does to individuals and marriages. He also added:

> Not long ago when I was in Orlando training on this very topic, I started off by saying that, "My hope today is that when you are finished with this class, you will no longer see this as a codependency issue. You will not see this as a relationship issue. You will see this as a betrayal trauma issue. You will see this as a trauma that looks a lot like post-traumatic stress disorder. This is my hope when you leave this class." This is a breach of the relationship, and this kind of trauma is just as real as any other type of trauma that could be experienced.

RECONSIDERING WORTHINESS AND THE PRIESTHOOD

In the Church, a "worthy" priesthood holder in the home and family is important in order to bless women and children. Many LDS women feel a worthy priesthood holder is an important criterion for marriage. Unfortunately, men being unworthy to use their priesthood, permeates many aspects of women's lives. Having their husband not be able to use his priesthood was also fraught with difficult and painful feelings. Wives became upset when their husband would use the priesthood unworthily or became deeply saddened when he could not use it to give blessings or perform ordinances like baptizing their child. The confusing and incongruent behavior of men using pornography and continuing to perform priesthood duties may confront women for the first time. Women shared how they felt unsure if they could even ask their husband to use his priesthood when pornography had been a problem and under what circumstances. There was also a question about the appropriate length of time between him viewing pornography and using his priesthood. Sarah told us when Hank first told her about his pornography use, that she was shocked when he passed the sacrament.

> We were sitting [in Sacrament meeting] and someone asked him to
> pass the sacrament. He got up and passed the sacrament. I remember I
> was shocked. I was ticked off. I was confused. He had looked at porn
> that Tuesday and was passing the sacrament on Sunday.

We heard stories of men who could not bless their baby or baptize their child because of their addiction. Those public instances of men not being able to use their priesthood caused deeply conflicted feelings for women: a sense of shame that he could not perform the priesthood ordinance; concern about what others, especially older children, were thinking; a sense of relief that he was being held accountable for using pornography; and a deep sadness that her husband seemed to choose viewing pornography over using his priesthood to bless his family. Claire shared her experience of her husband not being able to bless their new child.

> In the past, there has never been anything that he hasn't been
> able to do [with his priesthood]. They have never taken any [privileges]
> away. There have been times he shouldn't have blessed our kids, and I
> am grateful that he is not going to be able to bless this baby, but in a
> year he will be able to baptize his eight-year-old righteously because he
> will be able to take care of this problem. It will show that he is willing
> to sacrifice in order to overcome this addiction. So to me this is great
> and I don't really care about what anyone else thinks as long as he is
> working to get better.

Some women told us that they do not ask their husbands to give them priesthood blessings because they do not know if their husbands are worthy, or because they may harbor negative feelings toward their husbands. Instead, they ask another priesthood holder to give them a blessing or they forego the blessing altogether. Melanie spoke of her feelings about having a worthy priesthood holder in her home.

> Priesthood blessings are another big thing to me. I suffer from anxiety. There have been times when I have asked him for a blessing and he hasn't felt worthy to do it. This is really hard on me because I have always wanted a worthy priesthood holder in my home. Gratefully, we are moving forward to a time when he will always be able to do that for his family. He slipped not long before he blessed our baby. He said he felt he was in a place where he could still do it, but it really twinged my heart a bit. I just so badly want for me and my children to have a worthy priesthood holder in our home.

Alice shared the complex emotions she has about her husband using his priesthood.

> I have really lost a lot of respect for my husband. My philosophy with him has been to honor the good in him. Don't honor the other stuff that you worry about, just honor the good. I don't ask him for priesthood blessings anymore. I ask my bishop or my dad. My kids ask him, and I sit through it, and I know that even if he is not worthy, the Lord is not going to punish my kids because of it.

The issue of when men are worthy to use their priesthood is clearly complicated and of great concern to their wives.

COMFORTING RELIGIOUS WORSHIP BECOMES PAINFUL

Drawing closer to God and engaging more fervently in prayer, scripture study, and temple attendance become essential during difficult times. However, women experienced spiritual pain and distress from doing the very things that normally strengthened them when their lives had been shattered by their husband's pornography addiction. Temple attendance transformed from a place of peace to a source of dread and a reminder of broken covenants. It seems that women's spiritual pain only added to the betrayal trauma that they felt. Spiritual experiences that used to bring them comfort and hope seemed to become another source of their suffering. Sarah stated it this way:

I have always been very obedient and have always found peace and inspiration at church. However, attending church suddenly became confusingly traumatic for me. For months, talk about marriage, family, or "worthy priesthood holders" sent me crying to a church bathroom stall where I would spend sometimes over an hour trying to pull myself together.

The temple reminded women of the painful realities of their marriage. The endowment session and sealings were especially agonizing for women. These ordinances reminded women of temple covenants their husbands have made. Cynthia, whose husband had been using pornography and then had a one-night affair, shared her fears and pain about broken temple covenants.

> We were married in the temple. Since his disclosure, I have only been back once, and I only had time enough to do initiatories. It is scary to sit through a session and hear all of those covenants and the weight of it all and the seriousness of the ones he has broken. He has broken covenants that he has made before God, angels, witnesses, me, and [our] family. He has had Church disciplinary action taken against him, and I told him that once he gets all of his blessings and ordinances restored that it will still be scary because he made all these promises once and he flat out broke them.

At a deeper level, part of Cynthia's fear is related to the need for Thomas to restore trust in their relationship. Wives told us of the difficulty of going to the temple with their husbands because they wondered if their husbands were "worthy" to be there. Alice shared with us her thoughts about going to the temple with her husband.

> We have agreed that we wouldn't do an endowment session together. I respect that if he is lying to go to the temple that it is between him and the Lord. It is not for me to worry about. He will be the one that will pay for it.

Other wives whose husbands had lost their temple recommends found it unsettling to have a partner who is not on the same spiritual level as they are. Melanie shared,

> As far as the temple goes, there have been times when I go alone and I don't mind it. It is the thought that he can't go that really bothers me. Emotionally and spiritually this is hard, because I want a partner

that is on the same level as me and someone I can share these things with.

Some women stayed in their marriages because of covenants that were made in the temple, even though it was unclear to them if the covenants were still valid. The women we interviewed took temple covenants very seriously, but the reality of pornography use in their marriage caused women to acknowledge that their husbands needed to do their part. Alice's thoughts about ending her marriage mirror those of other women.

> I went from this perfect family, this perfect marriage, and living with a spiritual, loving husband that was a temple-goer to a husband who doesn't have his temple privileges. I know my Heavenly Father would never question my decision [about staying in my marriage] because He knows me. He knows where I struggle and He knows where I am strong. I am not afraid to get a divorce if that is what I need to do. But I also know that the biggest reason why I stay is because of the temple, because of covenants. It is a three-way relationship, and the Lord has not broken his covenants with me. I also still see good in my husband. I know that the day that I don't, that will be the day I leave. I tell him all the time that I hate that I love him so much. The last time I went to the temple with my husband was during the dedication of the temple. I was holding our daughter Taylor as we stood in the celestial room, and I looked in the mirrors that represent eternity. I thought to myself, *Ew, do I really want this? Do I really want this hard marriage? Do I really want to take this dysfunctional family into eternity?*

Attending Sunday meetings can be considered one way of finding peace and inspiration to deal with life's challenging issues, including living with a pornography addiction in a marriage. However, Church meetings, as indicated previously, had the potential, for many reasons, to be a difficult experience for women who were dealing with pornography in their marriage. Attending Church could be a reminder that they did not receive certain blessings they had expected to receive from living righteously. They felt virtually alone in dealing with the problem when they were attending church. Certain callings caused women some difficulty. They also perceived the talks and discussions about pornography as painful and not helpful because it did not focus on the day-to-day, painful realities of living with pornography in their marriage.

About half of the women we interviewed told us how as young women they dressed modestly, kept the commandments, and had high-quality friends. Almost all of the women we interviewed were married in the temple, and several women had served missions. Because they did these righteous things, they expected and sought after men who they believed did not have serious problems, especially with pornography. Sarah said that she had always tried to live a righteous life and follow all the "rules" that were supposed to "guarantee" a good husband and a good marriage. Courtney shared how unfair and difficult it was to have a pornography addiction be a part of her marriage:

> I was in a very normal Mormon family, and I was taught very early on that if you do good things, good things will happen to you. If you obey the law of chastity, if you dress modestly, you will attract the kind of people you want to have in your life. If you get married in the temple, you will have those blessings of eternal marriage and be able to work through hard things. I fully expected us to go through challenges, but I thought they would be challenges like we would not have enough money, or we would lose a job, or someone would get sick, or you know, we would lose people or things that mattered to us. But it never, ever, occurred to me that "we" might be the problem. That he might hurt me, that I might hurt him. That was just not an option; it never occurred to me. So I was kind of blindsided by that. I realized that all of the pain in my life was coming from my marriage relationship, which was supposed to be perfect because we got married in the temple, and because we didn't have sex before we got married, and because we did all of the right things. We did all of that. So I felt a little bit robbed, like I had been lied to almost, that "I did my part and this sucks." It's not fair. It just felt really, really unfair to me!

Cynthia expressed her perspective:

> When we first got married I was so grateful that I had done so many things right like living the law of chastity and serving a mission. So learning about this pornography problem was really hard for me to deal with because I felt like I had done all the things that God wanted me to do. But I still had to deal with this! It is really confusing to me that people can have such a strong testimony and be so active and be doing so many good things with their lives while being involved in such a dark, dark thing. You grow up being taught that if you live righteously and make good choices that you will be protected from

things like this. It is confusing to see that my husband was making a lot of good choices, but at the same time there were such horrible and evil choices going on.

For most women, their husband's pornography use was invisible to ward members. At times women felt like they were living a double life, where they pretended all was well in their day-to-day lives and even at church, despite knowing the pornography addiction was a major problem in their life. Some women found that because they did not feel like they could openly discuss their husband's pornography problem with others at church, they felt emotionally isolated from fellow Saints. When women cannot talk openly about this issue at church, it may feel to women like they are pretending that everything in their life is okay or that they are hiding who they really are. When Alice learned of Shawn's pornography addiction, her anorexia symptoms flared. The praise that Shawn received from ward members for being so supportive of Alice was very ironic to her.

> Every once in a while, I was tempted to just shout [about Shawn's pornography addiction] from the mountaintops. "You think you know him. You think he is so wonderful and perfect, but you don't have a clue who he really is." He had received so much praise when I went into treatment for my anorexia. Everyone told him how brave and support- ive he was. They had no idea what the real issue was.

Some women told us Church disciplinary action makes it known to others in the ward or community that their husband has a problem with pornography. Liz describes the difficulty she had when her husband was released from his calling and could not use his priesthood.

> Having my husband be in a position of Church prominence, and then all of a sudden having him not able to do anything brought lots of pressure on me and my children. We were the topic of a lot of gossip and speculation both in the Church and in the community. We were being shunned by the people that should have been helping us. My kids didn't understand, and quite frankly, neither did I.

Serving in callings where women were required to teach about uncomfortable topics, such as eternal families or temple marriage, also exacerbated spiritual pain. Sarah told us about her experiences as a Young Women leader.

The theme that August [when Hank disclosed his pornography addiction] was eternal marriages and families. At Church, I would go into the bathroom during the second hour and sob in the bathroom stall and then pull myself together so I could teach about happy marriages the next hour. It was really, really traumatic. All of the girls are very obedient. They are not naughty. I've got the nicest young women. I'd look at them and think, *I was once you.* I wanted to say to them, "You're going to marry a porn addict."

Women also had to come to grips with the fact that sometimes their husband's callings were not always a reflection of their husband's worthiness. For Alice, it meant she had to rethink what it meant to have certain callings.

He would take a cab and go to these strip clubs on his mission. His companion was sleeping. He never got caught, and he never talked about it. He had the best mission president and he never talked to him about it. He was even the assistant to the mission president (AP). I have really had to step back and realize that you don't receive callings based on your righteousness. I just couldn't believe how he had fooled everyone! I thought that at some point the Spirit should have jumped in and said, "No, he shouldn't be AP! No, he shouldn't be the executive secretary!" But it does not happen like that.

Women shared their frustration about how discussing pornography in lessons and talks was not always helpful because of the way the addict or user is portrayed. Melanie talks about how condemning men who have a pornography problem does not always represent their husbands because they still have many strengths.

A sexual relationship in the LDS church is such a sacred thing. If your husband struggles with pornography, then some Church members might think you are just the most horrible person. I tell people all the time that if you took all of my sins and all the bad things I have done in my life and there were a way to tally all of my sins, I know mine would be greater than his. My husband is a great man—an amazing man. He deeply loves Christ and his Heavenly Father, and Satan had to throw something big at him to get him to do anything. All the men that I know, that are in this same situation, are great and amazing men just like my husband.

Sarah felt like it was not safe to talk about a pornography addiction openly and that discussions about pornography only focused on how bad pornography was, rather than helping people who have a pornography addiction know how to overcome it.

> In Sunday School, when we are talking about pornography, I feel like I'm going to explode. It doesn't feel safe at Church, being open about what I'm dealing with. I feel bugged that someone with cancer can talk about all their spiritual experiences they've had but I have to stuff it. I feel frustrated that I don't feel safe openly discussing pornography at Church when it is so prevalent! In my experience at Church, there is a lot of, "Avoid pornography or else you will become addicted and it will destroy you" talk, or "Pray, read your scriptures, and repent so it doesn't happen again" talk, and not much talk about resources and solutions to the many who are already addicted and to the many who do not realize that their porn problem is actually an addiction.

Courtney's comments focused on the importance of avoiding shame messages, since shame can be the root of a pornography problem.

> We're just such a shaming culture that everything is bad, and it might have just been my house, but it felt pretty widespread in the LDS Church. It felt pretty common that . . . we keep telling our kids that these things we're experiencing are bad. It scares me the way that we handle things. That worries me. But the only thing to do is to fix it, and the more people experience this, the healthier the ideas we will have about the shame and the sex, and all of those things. I kind of feel like it'll self-correct. I hope it will self-correct. The healthier we are, the better we are able to teach these concepts.

There is already so much shame surrounding your spouse's use of pornography. He experiences shame every time he views it, and especially afterward. He may have also been exposed to shaming messages as a child. He uses pornography as a way to cope with the shame. Shaming and humiliating your husband only multiplies the negative emotions for him and the marital relationship. Although it may be difficult, shaming and humiliating your husband must be avoided.

Next we hear Cynthia's story. Cynthia and her husband Thomas were apart for a few months while they waited for their house to sell. It was at the end of one particular week that she learned about her husband's pornography use when he confessed to having a one-night affair.

CYNTHIA'S STORY

Thomas and I have been married for ten and a half years. As far as I knew everything was fine. Looking back, I can see a few vibes that are obvious now. We had our moments, but I considered it all very normal. There would be times either before or after sex that something just felt off. I was never abused and I was never pushed to do things I was uncomfortable with, but sometimes it just felt really weird. Then there were certain ways that he would behave at times. He would become grumpy and pull away from the family.

About four years ago, things really started to get hard for Thomas at work. He really pulled away, and I have felt like a single parent the past four years. I always just thought it was due to his stressors at work, and I understand that sometimes you just need to come home and unwind. Now I know that at this time he was just sinking further into his addiction.

So last year—almost exactly a year ago—he got a new job. It was three hours away from where we were living, so the plan was that he would work there during the week and come home on the weekends while I tried to sell the house. The house didn't end up selling until last September, so this past summer was really rocky. Thomas didn't really want to talk on the phone at night. He would never ask how I was doing, and he seemed to be getting angrier and angrier all the time. I actually got to the point that I didn't really care if he came home or not because we were not happy. Our relationship would just kind of go down and then it would come back up, but I never did realize how far down we were going. At the end of October, he told me he was going to work through the weekend and then come home on Saturday instead of Friday.

Then that Saturday morning Thomas called me and said that he was on his way home and that he had something to tell me and that it had to be face-to-face. He told me to take the kids somewhere because it needed to be just us and that I was to say a lot of prayers because I was going to need them. I told him that he was scaring me, and he said he was sorry but it is what it is. We have four boys and I took them to my best friend's house. I cried on her front porch and told her that I didn't know what was going on. I remember that my phone had been charging next to my dresser on the floor in my bedroom and so I was sitting on the ground when I was talking to him, and as I put my phone down I remember thinking what could possibly have happened that he has to come all the way back and miss the event that he was going to work at. I thought, *Did somebody die? Did somebody in his crazy family do something?* And then the Spirit just told me that Thomas had done something really, really bad. But I kept thinking, *No, no, no, no, no. He is a smart man. He is a good guy. He did not do anything really bad, that couldn't possibly be it.* But I kept being told that for the next three hours.

Well, Thomas finally came home. He came inside and sat me down on the couch and took a few deep breaths and he proceeded to tell me a variety of sins starting with adultery, addictions, strip clubs, and masturbation. He just dumped it all out. The hours that followed I had myriad emotions. One surprising one was that of peace, because I finally had some missing pieces of the puzzle that made the rest of our marriage make sense. But mostly it was just shock. I am still trying to deal with the trauma that is involved.

His first exposure to pornography was when he was six. Then he doesn't remember many details why, but he remembers when he was fifteen and the Internet was a big thing he remembers trying to convince his parents to get the Internet because he knew this was a way he could get the pornography. He knows at that point that he was already addicted. He is thirty-five now, so it has been at least twenty years.

Sitting there on the couch after he told me, I felt like I was going crazy because at that same moment I wanted to run across the room and kick him in the shins, then jump out the window and never come back. But I also wanted to hug him and tell him how sorry I was for all the struggles he has had for years and years, and sorry for all the pain it has caused. I felt split in a million different ways. I have felt those mixed feelings over and over again since then.

It has only been in the last five years that Thomas said that he really realized that this is an addiction. Prior to that he thought it was just a problem of being unclean minded and that guys did it and that he should just stop it. In the last two or three years is when it really escalated. This is when the strip clubs really started coming into the picture. He was scared at not being able to get a handle on things. He also knew that he would eventually get to the point where he would be seeking out real people. He didn't act on this until last June when he signed up on a website dedicated to helping married people have affairs. He didn't actually seek anyone out until October. They wrote to each other for a week. They met up on Friday night, and then he came home on Saturday.

Since that time, my thoughts centered on how worthless I felt. I didn't blame myself. Thankfully after he spilled out all of the horrible things that he had done, he told me that this had nothing to do with me. He has never tried to blame me for any of this. In the world that I live in, if you love someone and someone loves you and you said that we are going to go down this path together, that should be enough to keep you loyal, but apparently, it wasn't. I have tried to make sense of this, and the only thing that I could match up was me. If I was enough he wouldn't have met her, he wouldn't have wanted to go seek out someone else.

I have realized that the pornography played a major part in leading up to the affair. The affair though is the one thing that still hurts the most. But as I have come to understand more about his pornography use it hurts almost as much as the affair. It is basically cheating.

Sometimes I cry over the loss of what I thought I had. I cry to get all the pain out in hopes that I won't have to feel it anymore. I had a nice long crying session yesterday that I hadn't had in a few months, so I am actually feeling quite a bit better today.

Some days I feel like I could handle it if he slipped, but there are other days that I feel like I would break and punch him in the stomach. I guess it just depends on where I am emotionally. I have told him that I do want to know within twenty-four hours if he slips. I feel like I have a right to know, whether or not he thinks I can handle it. If you slip, I will make you sleep in the guest bedroom for a week or until I feel safe again. The most specific boundary I set is if he has another affair it outlines how long he has to be gone for and how long before he can see the kids. Also, we have a six-year-old, and I told him that he needs to be worthy to baptize him when he turns eight but I haven't come up with a consequence for that yet.

The principle of chastity feels more like a protection than I ever thought before now. Before it seemed to be more of an obedience thing. But now I realize that Heavenly Father set up this principle for us because He knew that having a body would set up all kinds of challenges for us, especially men, and if we follow these guidelines and principles we will have protection and we will be safer. We will be protected from the fiery darts of the adversary and we will be happier.

It has always been easy for me to wear what I am supposed to wear, and it is easy for me to throw out thoughts that come in that are not supposed to be there. When I see a handsome guy walk by, I think, *Wow, that guy looks nice!* and then I automatically think that I shouldn't even go there. I understand that those thoughts come for both men and women, but some people just have a harder time getting rid of them. For men the desires are so high, and for women we feel like that is the only power that we have. It is really easy to slip into a mind-set of immodesty because it feels like there is power and attention that we get from dressing that way. It stems not only from the bareness of clothing, but the tightness as well. It also causes an attitude that we have when we are wearing such clothes. I just feel like the world has set us up to fail in this regard.

I definitely feel like there are still some things that are too painful to talk about. I have found that there is a lot of healing power in just saying things, but I have also found that my husband is still at a point where things are all about him. He does acknowledge how hurt I have been and how I feel, but when I tell him that I am struggling or that something is really bothering me, that just brings up a lot of negative emotions inside of him. He blames himself and then he is left to feel like this really horrible person, so this makes it really hard for me to share my feelings. I find myself holding back a lot of things because right now I cannot handle those days filled with his negative emotions.

There are two people I feel safe talking to about this, but I just don't like burdening them with this. It is really hard. There are some things that I will talk to them about, but there are other things that I just keep to myself. I am getting to a point with my counselor that I can share some things that I don't share with anyone else. A lot of the time, I just come off as happy and that I'm doing just fine—anytime I talk to my parents on the phone, anytime we go visit family, anytime we are at church. I keep it from my parents to protect them and him. They love Thomas and they are proud of him and I don't want to take that away. He doesn't want to tell them either. He respects them a lot and telling them would be as hard for him as it was telling me. I don't want to tell them without his permission either. I know the feeling of having this picture of what he is destroyed, and I don't want them to have to experience that.

Thomas's brother and his brother's wife divorced over six years ago. When I found out about the divorce my eighteen-month-old son (my oldest) and I were in the car. I turned around and promised my son that his parents would never get a divorce. Over the past seven months I have come to realize that I cannot make that promise. I can promise him that I will always be there for him, and I can promise him that his parents love him, but I realize that I have zero control over what my husband chooses and thus no control on the way my marriage goes. I do realize that I can give my best effort in trying to make it what I think is a good marriage, but the outcome is determined wholly by how both people in the marriage contribute to a happy marriage.

At times I become really frustrated over how Thomas has used his agency and I have had to go through all of this because of *his* choices not mine. I feel more shafted than trapped. His misuse of agency has caused a tremendous amount of pain. The betrayal, the lies, and the questions about what the future holds, has caused me such pain. The security is all gone, but I guess it was never really there in the first place. In a way, it is good because now I have my feet on solid ground instead of my pretend world and the false safety that I perceived to be there. I suppose I should be thankful for that. His choices have definitely led me to open my eyes wider to what the world really is, and what my own pathway should be.

There has actually been a deeper level of intimacy since Thomas told me about the pornography and affair. Now that he has really opened up all of himself to me, we definitely have had a deeper connection. We are each bringing a lot more vulnerability to our relationship. In some ways, physical intimacy has become easier and in other ways more difficult. There is more passion involved because we are more connected, but there are also things that I won't come within ten feet of. There are still times that we are together and I feel like I am being attacked by thoughts of, *Is he thinking of her? Did she do this with him?* That is all very distracting, but for the most part it is better than it was.

Our biggest issue is that his go-to way of showing love is sex, and his way of feeling love is sex. That is fine with me as long as there are other things and other actions throughout the day. The emotional connections have somewhat faded out lately, and I feel more lusted after. We are currently trying to iron this out. I don't want to go down that path where I am not loved for all of me, just this part of me. But then he starts feeling unloved because I am withholding sex and that is his only way to feel loved. So I feel like we are always dancing around trying not to hurt each other's feelings, trying not to trigger trauma, and when we can make it past all of that then it is great.

We do better communicating in writing, as you can tell I have a hard time speaking what I am feeling, but I am able to write it. He and I sent a few emails back and forth yesterday about our sex life, and it was just too much. I also feel like I just get a handle on my life and this vast issue, and then that time of the month hits. I feel like I lose my grip on reality. It has been a week since he and I were last together, and he is desperately reaching out because he wants to feel loved, but I have been feeling that the only connection we have lately is sexual, so any kind of touch or anything like it makes me pull away.

When I start to think that I might not be the one Thomas wants anymore, I try to use a lot of positive affirmations and build my faith in the plan of salvation. I try to focus on the fact that this body is a gift and that it has done some pretty incredible things. The measure of my worth is not dictated by the firmness of my stomach. I just try and remind myself that I am a daughter of God, that He loves me, and He doesn't care what I look like as long as I am doing my best to take care of this gift that He has given me. It is so frustrating to be at this point where I am constantly having to talk myself out of thinking these negative thoughts about myself. I am frustrated that I am continually dealing with these thoughts because deep down I really know what the truth is. My husband has told me that he loves the way I look and that he loves my body. But I really think he says a lot of that because he knows it is the right thing to say rather than because he actually means it.

Forgiveness for me has been very confusing actually. When he first told me everything he moved off from the couch and onto the floor and stayed there for about an hour. I don't remember exactly what he said, but he started talking about forgiveness, and he said he knew that it was a lot to ask. He said he knows that it would help him a lot and me a lot if I could eventually forgive him, and the words just came out of my mouth, and I'm pretty sure they weren't mine because I said, "I forgive you, but trust and healing are going to take a lot longer." I think I shocked both of us with that, but it has been that way. I don't know why my journey with forgiveness has been different from others who I have talked with. It was just there. I didn't have to look for it; I didn't have to pray for it; I just know that it was the Savior that put those words in my mouth. He was the driving force behind my ability to forgive my husband.

I remember just shortly after Thomas disclosed the affair and his pornography use that a little video popped into my head. I was staring into this deep, dark chasm of awfulness, and I saw myself being snatched away from it by Christ. My eyes have been opened to how close to eternal sorrow we really come to as we have chosen to walk the path of mortality.

I know that if the Savior had not chosen to atone for us and if He had not been resurrected, I would be unhappy for the rest of my life because of the choices I have made and the sins that I have committed. The saving aspect of the Atonement has sunk in a lot more than ever before. He has rescued me. I know that in the premortal life I made a choice to come to earth and gain a body and take on the journey of mortality. I know that at that point I thought it was a pretty great idea and that it was something I was confident I could do. But the way in which we connect to each other in this life, and I assume in the life before and the life after, causes me to realize that we are a part of something bigger. It is really not in my power to get to where I want to be by myself. It is not in anyone's power to get to where they want to be by themselves. I have to rely on others, and I especially have to rely on Jesus to get to where I want to go.

Looking back, I now recognize that there wasn't much of the Spirit in our home most of the time. This experience has also taken my relationship with my Heavenly Father to a deeper level. I have only had to ask Him a couple of times, "Why? Is there no other way that we can do this?" I have never felt anger toward Heavenly Father for this trial, and I believe there are blessings that have come because of that. I have come in contact with all kinds of women who share this same trial, and I have seen the result of the choices they make in regards to Heavenly Father, and some of them are not even conscious choices. They experience a lot more anger, pain, and confusion, and it just looks a lot harder. I really don't know why I am different this way, why I haven't questioned or been angry with God. There just seems to be a lot more peace on my path. Perhaps it is just a blessing for some other choice I have made.

Looking back, I can only imagine that Thomas didn't want his four boys to end up in the same situation he found himself in. We have had several family home evenings (FHE) where he has taught lessons on pornography, and this was even prior to his disclosure. I look back and wonder what was going through his head at this time. FHE was always kind of tough to have because I felt like I was the one always dragging everyone into it, but whenever he would decide to talk about pornography he was gung ho. He was very intent on helping the boys understand. At the time, I remember thinking how nice it was to finally have him involved and excited about FHE.

Our oldest son just turned ten yesterday and last summer I started reading the book, *How to Talk to Your Child about Sex*. I thought that my husband and I needed to read this together so we could talk to our sons about it together. I gave him the book and told him to take it with him and that every night we would read a chapter together. I knew that if I read it to him he wouldn't listen. Well, he didn't read the book, and I don't even think he thought about it. So one of the first things we talked about after he disclosed to me was that we really, really needed to have the sex talk with our oldest son, but I no longer wanted to do it with him. I just don't think I could talk about this with our son with him there. So what we eventually worked out was that we had the talk with our son, but my husband was just on speaker-phone, and I did all the talking. I also want to get a book that has come out for younger children called *Good Pictures Bad Pictures* so that I can start talking to my other boys about pornography as well.

There have been a lot of messages in our stake over the past few years about the man's responsibility to lead his family in prayers, scripture study, and FHE. So it always felt wrong [taking over this responsibility], but I also knew that if I didn't do it, it wouldn't happen. I eventually just gave up. However, last summer I recognized that we needed something because we seemed to be down in a hole. It hit me again that we needed to be praying together and reading scriptures together so I started doing this with the boys before they went to school. We would call my husband and he would pretend to listen in and then we would say a little prayer. Thankfully that pattern had been established when things crashed with my husband, and he has been told by our stake president that he needs to be leading prayer, scripture study, and FHE, and that will be part of showing us that he is ready to come back into full fellowship of the Church. He is now serious about it. It gets done a lot more often, and I feel good about it.

I am so much stronger than I would have ever guessed. I was destroyed after hearing about the affair, but somehow I am still here. I am still living and breathing, and I am hopeful. This is how I know I am strong. The one thing that I thought would take me completely out, didn't. I attribute that to a lifetime of trying to make good choices and a loving and gracious Savior. Knowing Thomas's struggle is an addiction makes it easier because it helps me to see how he could have fallen prey to such things and how he could have made such choices. But it is harder because I still know that he made those choices. No matter what power Satan has with addictions, we still make choices.

The future of our marriage could go either way. I did have a strong, strong feeling that if he does leave I will be fine. I have great hopes for the future of my marriage, but the reality is, I really have no idea. I have hopes that our marriage can be stronger and that we can be happier. But I can also see how quickly it can go completely in the other direction. He can decide that it is too much hard work, give in, and leave. Either way, I am confident that I will be okay. It really is a hard pill to swallow when you realize that you don't know what the future of your marriage is.

CYNTHIA'S STORY AND SPIRITUAL GROUNDING

Cynthia's story clearly symbolizes how the spiritual truths upon which a marriage is established take a penetrating blow when pornography addiction is discovered, leaving the marriage and the spouse on very shaky ground. The discovery of a husband's addiction creates many painful and confusing emotions for women. Her thoughts and worries are split in a million different ways. Her concerns, questions, and confusion may first turn to her husband: *How could he have done this? He has broken sacred covenants. He is not a worthy priesthood holder. He is not going to be able to bless or baptize our children. Where does he stand with God?*

Her thoughts will then turn to their marriage: *Our marriage has been based on a lie. This temple marriage now means nothing. God told me it was okay to marry him. Is He punishing me? What is the future of our marriage, do I even want to be married to him? Does he want to be married to me?* And then finally, her thoughts will turn to herself: *How did I not see this coming? Am I incapable of receiving revelation or warnings from the Holy Ghost? Heavenly Father, are you really there? Why did you allow this to happen to me? I thought I was living worthy of your eternal blessings. What does this mean for my eternal salvation?*

These types of questions often run through a woman's thoughts until she is spiritually and emotionally exhausted. A wife will then wonder whom she can share this with, or if she should share it at all. She may turn to her bishop, ward members, family, or friends, only to realize their counsel was more harmful than helpful. Turning to her husband is also problematic because everything is still about him, and having to deal with his negative emotions on top of the addiction will be far too difficult. It was at this point that Cynthia prayerfully turned to her Heavenly Father. She felt His reassuring love and found great comfort in her knowledge of the plan of salvation. Her spiritual footing was once again restored and she found peace. Her example of prayer, fasting, and scripture study is invaluable to women who are also on spiritual shaky ground, for these will help in reestablishing a relationship with Heavenly Father. Through His Spirit, He can comfort and guide women through the difficult journey that still lies ahead. He can help women as He helped Cynthia, by allowing them to see their life as it really is. He can place them on the path they need to be on. A path filled with loving and trusted people, including the Savior, that leads to hope and healing for women. A path that will instill confidence in God, so that no matter what choices others may make, that everything will be okay.

Elder Jeffrey R. Holland so lovingly taught:

> I testify of angels, both the heavenly and the mortal kind. In doing so I am testifying that God never leaves us alone, never leaves us unaided in the challenges that we face. "[N]or will he, so long as time shall last, or the earth shall stand, or there shall be one man [or woman or child] upon the face thereof to be saved" (Moroni 7:36). On occasions, global or personal, we may feel we are distanced from God, shut out from heaven, lost, alone in dark and dreary places. Often enough that distress can be of our own making, but even then the Father of us all is watching and assisting. And always there are those angels who come and go all around us, seen and unseen, known and unknown, mortal and immortal.[69]

Heavenly Father loves His precious daughters and will never leave them. No matter what pain and heartache you may be experiencing now, and regardless of what the future may hold, you are never left to face this mortal journey alone.

6 HOPE AND HEALING

Hope is as essential to our happiness and well-being as the air we breathe. We must keep hoping and we must keep breathing if we are to stay alive.

— Ardeth G. Kapp[70]

True and lasting healing is possible for women who have endured the trial of pornography in their marriage. Whether or not their husband has chosen to become and stay sober, women need to heal in order to regain peace and hope in their lives. Women we interviewed sought many ways to heal. This chapter describes many types of healing, including healing that comes from relying on "the merits, and mercy, and grace" (2 Nephi 2:8) of Jesus Christ, which is ultimately necessary to reestablish hope and to completely heal. Shirley, whose story is at the end of this chapter, is an example of having Christ at the center of her healing and the foundation for her hope.

WHO NEEDS TO HEAL

Women we interviewed were initially concerned with, and at times even consumed with, their husband's healing. The women encouraged their husband to meet with priesthood leaders, professional counselors, or attend 12-step meetings; they also sacrificed their time and other resources necessary for his healing. However, the truth is that women are not responsible for their husband's recovery and healing or whether he recovers. And, no matter what their husband does, women need to heal from the trauma and betrayal they have personally experienced.

It can be counterproductive to think that if only the husband would become sober, the wife's wounds would heal. Alice accurately identifies that there are actually three things that need to be repaired:

> This is just my advice, but I would plead with the wife to start working on her healing immediately. Immediately! It is a long road and I waited and waited for years, doing things that were completely contradictory to what I needed to do to heal. I put my own healing on hold to "help" Shawn get better. I wish I would have realized early on that I was not the cause of my husband's addiction, and I also wasn't the solution for him getting better. I also wish I would have realized that there were three different things that needed to heal—myself, Shawn, and our marriage. All three things are separate from the other. I thought that if my husband was fixed, then that would fix me and our marriage. I was wrong. My husband's addiction recovery is separate from my marital relationship and my own betrayal trauma. Just because he is sober, doesn't mean I can trust him or that my triggers will disappear. I really believed that all three of these things (our marriage, my healing, and his recovery) would all just be fixed at the same time, but they are all completely different.

Courtney emphasized that women must focus on transforming and bettering themselves and not their husbands:

> This is not a walk in the park, but the Lord can use it to transform you. Especially as women, whether our spouses decide to overcome it or not, we can use this to build ourselves and our strengths, and learn from our weaknesses. The biggest thing that we need to work on as women or as parents is to keep bettering ourselves. Women are born to be nurturers, and because of this we want to fix everybody. The bottom line is we can only work on fixing ourselves. We cannot carry our husbands; we have to let the Lord carry them.

At first, Courtney really struggled with the concept that because of her husband's addiction she had been adversely affected in many ways and needed to heal as well. Even though he was the cause of all of her pain, it still came down to her behavior, her reactions to Randy, and her relationship with God. Courtney's healing journey was finally able to start once she realized that she had to let go of controlling Randy's healing and focus only on her own. Amber also realized the blessings of letting go of her husband's healing and focusing on her life. She said, "I have taken charge of my own life, my own testimony, and my relationship with my Savior. I am now focused on setting a good example for my girls of what a strong daughter of God looks like."

Just after learning about her husband's pornography addiction, Courtney really struggled with being truthful with herself about the effects Randy's addiction was having on her and her marriage. Once she allowed herself to see the truth of her situation, her healing journey was finally able to begin. She illustrated it this way:

> People would tell me, "You've got to work on you, you've got to figure out your own stuff, you've got to do all of those things," and then I would think to myself, *I wouldn't have stuff to work on if it weren't for him.* How can you say in the same sentence, "You didn't cause it, you can't control it, and you can't fix it," and then turn around and say, "But you need to fix yourself?" But finally, after being able to see him in my mind more as Christ sees him, seeing him through holier eyes, I was able to let go of him and work on me. I had heard all of this a thousand times, but none of it made sense until I felt it. Being able to work through all of that and to see him again as a human being and not as a monster or a crazy psycho, or whatever, but seeing him for who he really was, allowed me to finally work on me. I am finished judging him and I am trying really hard to be finished judging me. That is what allows me to move forward and heal.

Alice, on the other hand, is still striving to heal herself completely even though her husband is currently experiencing sobriety. In regards to the importance of establishing the truth about the effects of Shawn's addiction, she said:

> One thing that has surprised both my husband and me is that his sobriety hasn't "fixed" us. We both thought that sobriety from the addiction would make everything "better." But as we have learned (with the help of our therapist), the pornography addiction isn't the main problem that our marriage and I need to heal from. It is the betrayal, the lies, and the deceit. Even though my husband has been sober, he is still just learning how to be honest and transparent in our relationship. I find that I am pretty terrified of my husband—I am afraid that he will hurt me, betray me, or lie to me. I find that I am constantly worrying that I am living in a false reality that my husband

has created for me. It is a terrible place to be, but it is a part of the process and I know if I keep working that I will get through it, regardless of what my husband chooses.

Alice learned that the feelings of betrayal and the lies are the most challenging problems. This is likely the case in all marriages where pornography is involved. Alice at this point has chosen to stay with her husband in hopes that she, her marriage, and her husband will eventually heal. Other wives may choose to leave their marriage based on individual circumstances. Dr. Skinner has advocated that regardless if women choose to stay in the relationship or leave, working through the trauma is crucial. He stated:

> I think it would be naïve to say that the trauma just goes away with divorce. I've had some experience in this area, and I have discovered the false notion of, "So now that I have removed myself, the trauma is no longer present or gone from my life." Trauma doesn't heal that way. Trauma heals through resolving and working through whatever the issue or issues are.

Healing from trauma is very difficult because there doesn't seem to be a one-size-fits all solution and each woman is going to respond differently to the lies and betrayal in her relationship. Each woman's pain and suffering will be unique to her and her own lived experience.

While wrestling with the trauma they were experiencing, many of the women found themselves questioning how a loving God would allow them to suffer so much, especially when their husbands' choices were the primary cause of their suffering. Eventually however, many came to realize that the Savior cares about their individual growth and development. Understanding and having faith in the plan of salvation becomes crucial as we realize we came to earth to be tried and tested. It is through our experiences and trials that we are becoming more like Him. Our Savior's love and support are constant and abiding. He will provide strength for us, enabling us to endure suffering. In a familiar hymn, we are reminded that throughout our mortal journey He will help us:

> Fear not, I am with thee; oh, be not dismayed,
> For I am thy God and will still give thee aid.
> I'll strengthen thee, help thee, and cause thee to stand, . . .
> Upheld by my righteous, omnipotent hand.

When through fiery trials thy pathway shall lie,
My grace, all sufficient, shall be thy supply.
The flame shall not hurt thee; I only design . . .
Thy dross to consume and thy gold to refine.[71]

As each woman embarks on her healing journey, she will also readily discover that regardless of the source of pain and suffering, healing is hard work, and it is going to hurt. Speaking about the trials and suffering that are inherent in mortality, Dr. Elaine S. Marshall taught that, "Healing really only begins when we face the hurt in its full force and then grow through it with all the strength of our soul. For every reward of learning and growing, some degree of pain is always the price."[72] Dr. Marshall also believes that in order for healing to start, the hurt must be fully acknowledged and one must be willing to experience it. Women who are suffering might find strength in knowing what *New York Times* columnist David Brooks has observed about those who suffer:

> People in the midst of difficulty begin to feel a call. They are not masters of the situation, but neither are they helpless. They can't determine the course of their pain, but they can participate in responding to it. They often feel an overwhelming moral responsibility to respond well to it.[73]

As women seek to understand their pain and how they could possibly respond well to it, they will come to realize that their suffering and its required healing is also a very private endeavor, as the words of this hymn suggest, "In the quiet heart is hidden sorrow that the eye can't see."[74] We alone must bear our cross. Elder Neal A. Maxwell explained:

> There is, in the suffering of the highest order, a point that is reached—a point of aloneness—when the individual (as did the Savior on a much grander scale) must bear it . . . alone. Even the faithful may wonder if they can take any more or if they are in some way forsaken.
>
> Those who . . . stand on the foot of the cross often can do so little to help absorb the pain and the anguish. It is something we must bear ourselves in order that our triumph can be complete.[75]

If the Savior is involved in healing, it can become sacred healing. By embracing the power of Christ's Atonement, the heartache, suffering, and disappointment from a husband's pornography addiction can be healed.

Dr. Marshall taught:

> Healing involves a private personal communion with the Savior, the Master Healer. It inspires a very personal reverence and awe. While on the earth Jesus often healed in private and then departed. When He healed, He often charged, "See thou tell no man; but go thy way" (Matthew 8:4; see also Luke 8:56).[76]

HEALING FROM BETRAYAL TRAUMA

Healing from betrayal trauma can be a long and arduous journey, but is one that must be taken. During the interview with Dr. Skinner, we asked what women needed to do to heal from betrayal trauma. He said that the answer is quite complex, and there are many ways and different experiences that can help them to heal.

> The first thing we look at in helping people resolve betrayal trauma is dealing with their images or memories associated with the trauma. Then we look at specific beliefs that they have come to believe about themselves; the beliefs that have come about because of the betrayal trauma. Those beliefs typically sound something like this, "I'm not lovable. It's my fault. I'm not good enough. If I were better, he wouldn't have to do this." Along with, "There must be something wrong with me. I have flaws. Nobody else would love me. I deserve it." Those types of beliefs, if you listen to them, sound hopeless. When a person has their memory along with their beliefs that they are not good enough, the emotions that come with it are sadness, anger, a sense of deep loss. We look at the images and the memories, the beliefs, and the emotion, and then the next part of the healing is the physical sensations such as, "How is my body influenced by the intensity of this stress (which is often overlooked in this process)? If you live in constant fear of what your spouse is doing, you are getting more cortisol and adrenaline because you are in the fight or flight mode. The consequence of being in the fight or flight mode is that you don't get to a calm stage, which has many implications for how our body functions. It means that you stop digesting food, you don't sleep as well, and your body's immune system gets attacked because it doesn't have the energy to fight off common illnesses. These are all a result of being in constant stress. From my perspective, we have to do all of those things to help resolve the trauma.
>
> Let's just take the first part of this, when you deal with treating the beliefs that are associated with the trauma. I look at how the beliefs

are formed, "I wasn't good enough, or I wasn't this, or I wasn't that." In therapy we have to look at and dissect those beliefs so women can understand the situations where those beliefs were established. I take the approach of helping them reorganize and reorient them into new beliefs.

There are many ways you go about healing from the trauma—talk therapy, Eye Movement and Desensitization and Reprocessing (EMDR) therapy, mindfulness, writing about it, and understanding those elements that I just talked about. We must literally use all of those tools to navigate step-by-step through the trauma, beliefs, physical sensations, and images that are the most haunting or difficult to deal with. I am a big advocate of having a team approach rather than an individual approach. So helpers could include: religious leaders, family members, therapists, 12-step groups, and sponsors.

Many of the women we interviewed acknowledged the benefits of implementing the tools that Dr. Skinner and other qualified professionals have recommended. They also shared the difficulty of the healing journey and recognized that much of the healing work was accomplished alone—secretly and sacredly inside their own heart (this is reminiscent of Mary, the mother of Jesus, and how she "kept all these things, and pondered them in her heart" (Luke 2:19)). This did not, however, diminish the loving and compassionate help they received from others along their healing journey. Dr. Skinner advocated having a team of support, and he also suggested ways that others can help women heal who have pornography in their marriage.

I think the very most important thing for every one of us is simply to feel understood. The best response may be no response. Women just want to be understood. You don't have to judge them or their situation; you don't have to do anything but try to understand their suffering. True compassion is being with someone in their suffering. So I believe that the other person's role is not to fix it, it is not to give them advice (unless it is solicited), but it is much more effective to just help them feel understood.

I think that this is something that is done step-wise and not instantly. Part of it is that they get back to a feeling that God loves them by connecting with other people. Someone may show them some mercy or give them love, and because they were given love, they then realize, "I am lovable!" Or as a couple they may start to work through the healing and recovery, and they see the hand of God (and the love of God) in their individual healing and recovery. There is not just one way to feel love from others. Sometimes there is a religious leader that says "Hey, I support and care about you," and that really helps. Sometimes there is a friend, a neighbor, or someone in a religious setting such as a visiting teacher or a Relief Society president who recognizes that it is fundamental that we all need to feel loved. We all need to feel loved. There are other times when women fast and pray, and they feel the sweet power of God's love and His affirmation that they are going to be okay.

THE HEALING POWER OF THE ATONEMENT

Having faith in the Lord Jesus Christ and His Atonement is the first principle of the gospel, and for a good reason. It is through the exercise of this faith, coupled with obedience and diligent seeking, that one can access grace and begin the healing journey. While not explicitly referring to healing from the impact of pornography, Elder Richard G. Scott has beautifully taught us how the ultimate healing must come from the Savior.

> No matter what the source of difficulty and no matter how you begin to obtain relief—through a qualified professional therapist, doctor, priesthood leader, friend, concerned parent, or loved one—no matter how you begin, those solutions will never provide a complete answer. The final healing comes through faith in Jesus Christ and His teachings, with a broken heart and a contrite spirit and obedience to His commandments. . . . The Lord will give relief with divine power when you seek deliverance in humility and *faith in Jesus Christ*. . . . No one can help you without faith and effort on your part. Your personal growth requires that. Don't look for a life virtually free from discomfort, pain, pressure, challenge, or grief, for those are the tools a loving Father uses to stimulate our personal growth and understanding. As the scriptures repeatedly affirm, you will be helped as you exercise *faith in Jesus Christ*. That faith is demonstrated by a willingness to trust His promises given through His prophets and in His scriptures.[77]

According to the Hebrew lexicon, the English word "Atonement" is translated from the ancient Hebrew word "kaphar," which means "to cover."[78] Through Jesus's atoning sacrifice we are *covered* emotionally and spiritually. Jesus *covers* us when we feel worthless and inadequate, lost and discouraged, abused and hurt, defenseless and abandoned.[79]

Many of the women we interviewed expressed the fact that even though they prayerfully sought different avenues of healing, it was a more complete understanding and application of the Atonement that allowed them to experience true healing. Courtney said this about the healing of her betrayal trauma symptoms:

> I can't give credit anywhere but to the Atonement for [healing]. . . .
> I don't want to discount the work that I have done and the information
> that I have received from experts, because that is huge. But in all hon-
> esty, I have read a lot of books, I have spent a lot of time in therapy, and
> I have tried to work through my emotions before. None of it has done
> any good until [I applied] the Atonement. I can't give credit to anyone
> or anything other than God.

Wives of pornography addicts are in desperate need of the Savior and His atoning sacrifice. Alice expressed it this way: "I don't know if I can describe it other than to say that without it, I would have given up on everything I ever believed in. I would have walked away, disappeared, and given up completely. The Atonement is the only way that I survived."

While Dr. Skinner has a great deal of knowledge and skill in helping women heal, he clearly testified that true healing comes from God and His Son's Atonement.

> I do not know how people can heal without an understanding
> of the healing power of God. This doesn't mean that a marriage will
> necessarily get better; it means that you will feel the power and love of
> God in your life. I do not know we can heal long-term without Him.
> We can turn to other things, but there is only one source of true and
> lasting healing power. I firmly believe that He is the healer, and when
> we try and heal without Him in our lives, we are almost always going to
> fall short of that and feel like we are missing something. I believe that
> God has that power for us as His children.
>
> The Atonement is a process where we come to rely upon God,
> not just concerning our sins, but our infirmities as well. He healed the
> blind; He healed the sick; He healed the lepers. If He could heal them,
> can He not heal us with our emotional wounds?

There are many key components to healing, but in the end, it is important to remember that ultimate healing comes from our Savior

Jesus Christ. It is a sacred gift bestowed upon each of us that often requires effort and even suffering on our part. In His wisdom and love He allows for such struggles so that growth and development can occur. One person's healing journey will look different than someone else's. Healing does come in its own time, its own way, and by His grand design. Elder Dallin H. Oaks taught:

> Healing blessings come in many ways, each suited to our individual needs, as known to Him who loves us best. Sometimes a "healing" . . . lifts our burden. But sometimes we are "healed" by being given strength or understanding or patience to bear the burdens placed upon us.[80]

THE SAVIOR KNOWS HOW TO SUCCOR US

When women are suffering at the hand of their husband's pornography addiction, it is important for them to realize that the Savior is intimately aware of their suffering, for he has taken their suffering upon Himself, and He is eager to rescue them. Elder Holland has spoken of the Savior's "brotherly hands and determined arms that reached into the very abyss of death to save us from our fallings and our failings, from our sorrows and our sins."[81] Similarly, the Book of Mormon prophet Alma taught:

> For behold, the time is not far distant that the *Redeemer* liveth and cometh among his people. And he shall go forth, suffering pains and afflictions and temptations of every kind; and this that the word might be fulfilled which saith he will take upon him the pains and the sicknesses of his people. And he will take upon him death, that he may loose the bands of death which bind his people; and he will take upon him their infirmities, that his bowels may be filled with mercy, according to the flesh, *that he may know according to the flesh how to succor his people according to their infirmities*. (Alma 7:7, 11–12; emphasis added)

Elder David A. Bednar reaffirmed this very concept:

> The Savior has suffered not just for our sins and iniquities—but also for our physical pains and anguish, our weaknesses and short-comings, our fears and frustrations, our disappointments and discouragement, our regrets and remorse, our despair and desperation, the

injustices and inequities we experience, and the emotional distresses that beset us.[82]

Shirley shared this insight into the Savior's ability to succor us:

> I have learned that a central part of the plan of salvation was that there had to be a Redeemer provided. It is because of Jesus Christ and His Atonement that I am able to hang on to hope, and that I have faith rather than fear, and that one day my husband will be able to partake of all of those same blessings. But it will be on the Lord's timetable and not mine. . . . The Atonement isn't just meant for someone who is steeped in sin but for me. It is the succoring powers of the Atonement. I truly have felt my Savior in my heart lifting me up, comforting me, and carrying me. While this trial has been devastating for me, at the same time I am really starting to appreciate it as a blessing. Because of this trial, I have a more in-depth understanding of the Atonement, more so than I have ever had before. It has been humbling, and I find myself a lot less judgmental of others. I have become a lot more merciful myself, and I am gaining greater qualities that I know my Heavenly Father wants me to have.

When women put their faith and trust in Jesus Christ they will begin to recognize that because He has suffered all things, He knows how to succor and heal them. He knows every tear that women have cried, every heartache they have felt, and every worrisome fear and uncertainty they have experienced. He also knows how to bind up every wound, mend every broken heart, and quiet every troubled thought and feeling. Elder Bednar also testified:

> There is no physical pain, no anguish of soul, no suffering of spirit, no infirmity or weakness that you or I ever experience during our mortal journey that the Savior did not experience first. You and I in a moment of weakness may cry out, "No one understands. No one knows." No human being, perhaps, knows. But the Son of God perfectly knows and understands, for He felt and bore our burdens before we ever did. And because He paid the ultimate price and bore that burden, He has perfect empathy and can extend to us His arm of mercy in so many phases of our life. He can reach out, touch, succor—literally run to us—and strengthen us to be more than we could ever be and help us to do that which we could never do through relying upon only our own power.[83]

The Savior also knows exactly what it is like to be betrayed by someone close. Judas Iscariot was one of Christ's original twelve Apostles. He was intimately familiar with who the Savior was and all that He had accomplished, and yet, for nothing more than self-gratification, Judas betrayed his Master with a kiss for thirty pieces of silver (see Matthew 26:14–16). This knowledge gives one confidence in turning to the Savior with full assurance that He knows and has experienced personally the pain of betrayal. Alice shared with us her empathy about Christ's betrayal.

> The Savior was betrayed by His best friend, and so was I. I find peace and comfort in knowing that the Savior can relate to my pain. The Savior didn't just experience the pain of sin, he experienced the pain of loving someone and having that someone hurt you, and I think he suffered even more for those types of things than he did for the sinner.

The women that we interviewed all confessed a belief in the saving power of the Atonement, the power Christ has to save them from sin and death. Many of them were also beginning to realize the Savior's redeeming power—the power and authority that Christ has to redeem them from the effects of living in a mortal world. President Dieter F. Uchtdorf taught that it is the saving power of the Atonement that unlocks the gates of Heaven, but it is the Savior's redeeming power that opens the windows of Heaven "through which God pours out blessings of power and strength, enabling us to achieve things that otherwise would be far beyond our reach."[84]

THE ENABLING POWER OF THE ATONEMENT

Christ's redeeming power not only comforts and heals us but also enables us to become even better than we were before. Courtney soon realized that she, her husband, and her marriage could not only be healed but could become even stronger than they were before the pornography.

> I felt like the Atonement to me was something that if you checked off all of these things on this list, and if you did everything right, then God would make up for your weaknesses; like for those teeny-tiny lapses in judgment. That if by chance one time you didn't do something right, that would be okay and you could be forgiven. Whereas now I believe that the Atonement is all of it. The Atonement is the only reason I can ever do anything good. The Atonement covers not just the

teeny-tiny lapses in judgment (which it does), but it also covers the heartache and the pain and the lost opportunities. I believe now that my relationship with Randy can be everything it would have been without the porn. . . . I feel like the whole point in life is to make mistakes and to figure out what we need to learn from them, because that is what give us strength and helps us to become more like Him.

Mormon scholar Robert L. Millet further illustrates this point:

> The Atonement does more than fix the mistakes. It does more than balance the scales. It even does more than forgive our sins. It rehabilitates, regenerates, renews, and transforms human nature. Christ makes us better, worlds better than we would have been had there been no Fall.[85]

One of the most important purposes of the Atonement is the enabling power that it gives us to not only overcome our weaknesses, but to develop the divine traits our Heavenly Father wants us to have. Christ Himself learned by the things He suffered in the flesh; "though he were a Son, yet learned . . . by the things which he suffered (Hebrews 5:8). The pain and suffering women have experienced because of their husband's addictions has been crippling and life-altering, but it is a great comfort to know that Christ suffered all things, and thus He knows perfectly how to succor and heal us. As this sacred healing takes place, according to Dr. Marshall, healing also teaches us:

> When we have a terrible loss or pain, we may seek to "get back to normal" or to the way things were before, but they will never be the same. Pain changes us, but not in the same way that healing teaches us. Healing can help us to become more sensitive and more awake to life. Healing inspires repentance and obedience. Healing invites gifts of humility and faith. It opens our hearts to the profound complexities of truth, beauty, divinity, and grace.[86]

Further, Orson F. Whitney wrote:

> No pain that we suffer . . . is wasted. It ministers to our education, to the development of . . . patience, faith, fortitude and humility. All that we suffer . . . , especially when we endure it patiently, builds up our characters, purifies our hearts, expands our souls, and makes us more tender and charitable, more worthy to be called the children of God . . . and it is through sorrow and suffering, toil and tribulation, that we

gain the education that we come here to acquire and which will make us more like our Father and Mother in heaven.[87]

It is the enabling power of Christ's Atonement that allows us to learn, grow, and develop as we are healing. As this healing takes place, inevitably there will be times of fear, frustration, and doubt. During these times it becomes crucial to stay focused on the Savior and His redeeming love. It is also well to remember Christ's question to a sinking Peter, after he had walked on the water: "O thou of little faith, wherefore didst thou doubt?" (Matthew 14:31). The moment Peter allowed doubt and fear to overtake him, he took his eyes off the Savior and severed himself from the very power that had sustained him on the water. It is important to not allow doubts, frustrations, and fears to sever the enabling power of God. (See D&C 6:36, 67:3.)

Grace is synonymous with Christ's enabling power[88] or the "divine help or strength . . . given through the mercy and love of God."[89] Sister Sheri L. Dew defines grace as "divine power that enables us to handle things we can't figure out, can't do, can't overcome, or can't manage on our own."[90] The grace made possible through Christ's Atonement is that same enabling power that allows us to *be* and *do* so much more than our finite minds can comprehend. According to Elder David A. Bednar, we, as members of the Church, struggle when it comes to accessing the Savior's grace:

> I suspect that [we] are much more familiar with the nature of the redeeming power of the Atonement than we are with the enabling power of the Atonement. . . . I frankly do not think many of us "get it" concerning [the] enabling and strengthening aspect of the Atonement, and I wonder if we mistakenly believe we must make the journey from good to better and become a saint all by ourselves through sheer grit, willpower, and discipline, and with our obviously limited capacities.[91]

"The doctrine of the grace of the Father and the Son and how it affects us is so significant that it is mentioned more than two hundred times in the standard works."[92] It is a doctrine that when fully understood allows for heavy burdens to be lifted, intense pain to be lessened, and overwhelming sadness to become much more bearable. It is Their grace that gives us strength enough to move forward.

There are multiple ways that we can access our Redeemer's grace, including praying, fasting, studying the scriptures, and worshipping in the temple. As we do these things, we will feel God's love and come to know that His promises are sure. Courtney shared with us that doing these things is not always easy, but when she does put forth an effort to do them, it makes all the difference.

> Staying active in the gospel is one of my main coping strategies. My biggest struggle is scripture study. I also struggle with formal prayer. I talk to my Heavenly Father all day, but I am not good at kneeling down morning and night. But when I do these things, I can really notice the difference. I also make sure that I attend the temple regularly. When I go there it really allows my brain to calm down. It also helps me to keep things in perspective. I have come to realize that just because we are doing all of the things that we should, such as temple attendance, scripture study, and prayer, that it doesn't mean that everything is going to be hunky-dory. But by doing these things, no matter what happens, they allow me to cope.

Other women, as noted in the previous chapter, found these same activities at times to be painful, depending on where they were in the healing process. Regardless of where women are in the healing journey, Sister Neill F. Marriott has offered these encouraging words,

> When we offer our broken heart to Jesus Christ, He accepts our offering. . . . No matter what losses, wounds, and rejection we have suffered, His grace and healing are mightier than all. Truly yoked to the Savior, we can say with confidence, "It will all work out."[93]

Your life, no matter how challenging it may be at times, *will all work out* as you come to better know your Redeemer and rely upon Him. Dr. Johnathan G. Sandberg, an LDS therapist and professor at Brigham Young University, also attests to this:

> I know that Jesus Christ is the great Healer. Over many years, in numerous settings, I have seen wounds of horrific abuse, long-standing addiction, loss that has shattered the soul, and heartache beyond description be addressed, overcome, and resolved through the Atonement of Jesus Christ. I know He is a real, living, loving God. I love and honor Him. I know His grace is sufficient—meaning big or powerful enough—to help us with all our problems. I know His promises to us are real and true. He can and will cleanse and heal us as He has said (see Ezekiel 36:25–28).[94]

Shirley shares with us her story about how her husband's pornography addiction shattered the life and dreams she and her husband had built together. After fruitless attempts to help her husband, she soon recognized she could not control her husband's addiction and needed to focus her energy on her own healing. Shirley's story illustrates the strength that comes from living the gospel of Jesus Christ, and the healing that takes place by trusting in the Savior, as well as the tools Heavenly Father has provided. Shirley is currently trying to use all available Church resources and is actively working on her recovery. She is hopeful that at some point her husband can do the same.

SHIRLEY'S STORY

My husband and I have been married twenty-five years and we have six children. We moved from the West to a rural community in the East. We moved here fourteen years ago, when our kids were all pretty little. There are a lot of blessings that come from living in a rural environment. When we first moved here, we experienced a lot of spiritual growth with our family because of our Church service, missionary work, and involvement in the community.

We have had some exterior stressors that came up in our lives in the past five or six years. All of the stressors came at the same time. In 2008 with the economic downturn, we experienced some financial setbacks. We had two missionaries out in the field. At the same time, one of our children had an illness. I remember thinking at the time that this was just too much. It was really stressful for me, and I know that it was also really stressful for my husband.

While we were experiencing all of the stressors, I really felt him start to emotionally pull away from me and the family. We had always been really close, but he just became more and more distant and wasn't quite himself. Our intimacy really suffered. We were going through all of these trials, but it didn't feel like we were going through them together. I didn't know why at the time, but I now know that is when he started looking at pornography. What I failed to realize is that when my husband was involved in pornography, he became emotionally abusive, and I didn't understand where that was coming from.

I got so busy taking care of everybody else that all of a sudden I became that person who just takes care of others. I look back now and realize I had really lost my identity, and it was made worse by the emotional changes in my marriage. From what I know now, it was when his pornography use started that his rudeness and emotional abuse started toward me. Over time I really started to believe the rude things he would say. I remember one time praying and just feeling the tremendous love that my Heavenly Father has for me, and I was reminded that I am a daughter of God. This began my pathway back to finding myself because I felt how much I was loved and cherished by my Heavenly Father. I really felt my worth for the first time in a very long time

I missed our partnership. My husband became more coercive and controlling. He was changing and was very different. I was trying to hold on to the way things used to be, and I didn't understand at the time what was really going on, what was really behind his behavior.

We sought counseling from an LDS counselor during this time. We only went a few times. My husband blamed his responses on my reactions and told the therapist that I had a mental illness or some kind of disorder, so therapy became focused on me. I thought, *Wait a minute! We are having marital issues, so why aren't we focusing on that?* This put me in a very defensive position and I withdrew from therapy. My husband was a bishop, and because of that, he had already established a relationship with the therapist, because he would refer ward members to this counselor.

All this time I did not know that the pornography was the real issue. My husband became almost obsessed with the idea that I had some type of mental illness or personality disorder. Several years later we attempted therapy again and it was still the same. I felt totally coerced by my husband, the male therapist, and the stake leaders who were involved. All the while my husband was the one viewing pornography and nobody knew it! I was the one experiencing the hurt and the betrayal! He was in such denial at that point that he would do anything to protect exposure of his pornography use. So again, therapy did not work out well.

At this point we just became really preoccupied with our children. One of our children got married. We had missionaries coming home and others leaving We just became locked up in the busyness of our lives. We just tabled the marriage issues and simply existed together.

Last summer we had one of those really busy summers. I was almost at the point of exhaustion. I still felt that there was something desperately wrong, but I did not know what. I decided to turn to the Lord for answers. I fasted, prayed, and went to the temple. As I sat in the temple, I just felt this overwhelming feeling that there was a problem. I can't describe how

I knew, but I just knew. I knew that it came from the Lord. I didn't have any reason to suspect pornography, but for some reason that was just put in my mind. So after this experience in the temple, I confronted my husband. I told him I wasn't sure what it was, but that I knew something was wrong and that I could not take the way things were anymore. I really felt like we were in a "do or die" situation. We were either going to end up apart or we were going to be together. At this point he did disclose to me that several years ago, during the initial onset of our family stressors, that he was exposed to pornography almost by accident on a business trip. He said that at first it wasn't a compulsion, but eventually he became addicted. He had tried to stop on his own but was unsuccessful. At this point he was completely powerless over it.

At the time he disclosed that pornography was the problem, I was feeling great compassion and love for him. He felt a lot of guilt and shame. He was crying and telling me how hopeless he felt, and I was bearing my testimony to him. I told him that it is never hopeless. It is not hopeless because of the Atonement. It was just a complete shock to me. I felt like it was a head-on collision. My life was a certain way one day, and I woke up the next morning and it was completely different. Since then, it has become a journey of learning to not be angry. Anger is not of the Savior, and it is not what He wants for us. I have really cycled through different emotions. I didn't know this was going to be a long-term problem. After the initial disclosure, he met with his priesthood leader. In between disclosing to me and meeting with the priesthood leader his story had completely changed. He was in denial mode.

Recently, we had an argument over a business decision. He became really angry about it and left. He stayed gone for a couple of weeks, but he would come and go. I kept telling him that this is too hard on me and the kids, and that he needed to make a decision one way or another. It got to the point that I finally removed the rest of his stuff and put it in the car. Since that point I have told him I want to reconcile, but now I realize that he was digging in his heels about his addiction. He couldn't cope with it around me and even around the kids.

We have since separated. He wants a divorce, and I do not want a divorce. He is so steeped in denial, and he still believes that I am the one who is crazy. We are just in limbo. We are not divorced yet. I know where we have been, but I do not know where it goes from here.

I knew he used his cell phone to view pornography, and I began trying to control his behaviors. I began to dictate how his recovery would go. That was wrong. He needed help, but I am not the help. You cannot control their addiction. You did not cause it, and you cannot cure it. At the time, we were attempting reconciliation, and it was hard because I would have good days and feel this great love for him, and then he would withdraw again. I knew those were the times he was unable to let go of pornography.

I quit eating, and I didn't really mean to—it was just from all the emotional trauma. I dropped a lot of weight really fast and so my doctor was quite concerned. I was just experiencing so much despair that I stopped taking care of myself. I just went into complete physical shutdown. President Uchtdorf talks about how despair is just this spiraling staircase that spirals forever downward, and it is hope that lifts us out of this. Our Father in Heaven knew that this was going to happen. He has given me the tools. I have all that I need to return back into our Father's presence. I just have to learn to trust Heavenly Father, trust His timetable, and trust that He has put those tools there for me and my children to deal with our trials.

I did seek counseling for myself, and one important thing my therapist said would be important for me was to have a good support system and to find safety. For me, mine and my husband's separation has been good because it has helped me with that emotional safety. I think it would be really hard to deal with him right now. Maybe the Lord knew that without my husband gone, I could not have found my own healing.

The Lord is in charge, and I have come to learn I was impatient. I also had poor reactions, and I did a lot of persecuting and blaming. Both of us did that. You call out each other's weaknesses, you blame them, and then you shame them. You think you can shame them into recovery, but it doesn't work. All it does is make them defensive, and then you are in this cycle of blaming and shaming and not finding any real answers. For me the separation has been at least a healthy time. I have been able to seek out recovery for myself. I have been able to find healing and to discover how to love him no matter what his choices are. Really that is where the focus is now. I need to focus on the Atonement and focus on love.

As I learn more and more about the nature of the disease, I take it less personally. I now feel like it is not an intimacy issue, but it is an addiction. In Sex Addicts Anonymous (SAA) and other 12-step programs you learn this. You learn that it is no longer about sex. It is no longer a reflection on you. You start to realize that your worth is no longer based on how your husband feels toward you, but on how much you realize your Heavenly Father loves you. I am no longer defined by what my husband thinks about me or by what his choices are. It has taken a while to get to this point, but this is where I am today. My worth comes from who I am as a daughter of God. I know that I am a modest and virtuous daughter of God, and I know that I have kept my covenants with Him. I know that I am loved. At the same time, I know that my husband is a cherished son of God, even though he is addicted to pornography. He truly is loved by the Lord.

I started attending a program sponsored by LDS Family Services called Healing through Christ. The manual is beautiful. As I started to focus on a recovery program for myself and how the twelve steps applied to me, the anger started to leave. In the beginning, I was focused on my husband and everything he should change and everything he should do. I learned that I needed to change my behaviors. It has been a spiritual journey. I used to base my moods on my husband's actions and what he thought of me, but now that is not what defines me. I have learned to detach in a loving way, and I am not allowing his moods and his choices to define my own happiness and well-being anymore. The healing journey has come as I have strengthened my relationship with my Heavenly Father, improved myself, and repented of the things that I have done wrong in our relationship. Truly, just reaching out and finding my Savior like I have never done before, I have become more understanding of His life and His teachings, and I have become more trusting of Heavenly Father. He has my husband, my children, and me in His care. In Doctrine and Covenants 100:1, it says, "Your families are well; they are in mine hands, and I will do with them as seemeth me good; for in me there is all power." At the beginning of my journey, I felt like I had some power, I felt like I had some control over the situation, and if I did things to help my husband and to help my children, that somehow this would improve the situation. But really I am learning exactly what it says in the scriptures: in the Lord there is all power. I don't have that power; only Heavenly Father has that power. In the 12-step program we have to admit that we are powerless over the addiction or the addicted loved one. Of course we are powerless, because Heavenly Father has all the power. He lends us breath from day to day. We are foolish to think that we have any power over any of this. Once we realize this and turn the power back to whom-ever it rightfully belongs, we in turn begin to rely more on Christ. So that has been my journey.

I do believe that my husband is capable of being honest and trust-worthy. There have been times in our marriage where I have definitely felt that. But how I look at it now is that when a person is caught in this disease and addiction, he is incapable of being trustworthy. It is like expecting a person who is paralyzed and in a wheelchair to get up and walk across the room. He simply isn't capable of it. If I am faith-ful and true with an honest heart to my covenants, then I am okay. My trusting relationship is not between my spouse and me; it is between my Father in Heaven and me. It really is an unrealistic expectation to place upon my husband right now. He cannot get up out of that wheelchair and walk across the room. He is going to have to deal with his disease in increments. And it will be on his terms, not mine.

Pornography has completely destroyed all types of intimacy in my marriage. My husband simply was not there. I felt it and I knew it. From a spiritual perspective, we built a life together. We built dreams together. We would kneel in prayer together and seek revelation. We were spiritu-ally connected, but then I felt him changing and withdrawing. I didn't feel preeminent in his life anymore. I felt like everything else was more important to him—his job, his calling, the kids, anything. There was no longer that time when we would have that spiritual moment kneeling at our bed in prayer, that spiritual and emotional union was gone. He really withdrew, and our relationship developed more of a lustful nature instead of that bonded spiritual relationship that true intimacy has. There were always times that I felt the Spirit so strong with him. He gave beautiful Spirit-filled blessings to me and my children. The loss was gradual and I didn't even realize it. Over the past four or five years I have felt that com-pletely diminish.

I have to really trust the Lord and His timetable. The Lord will seek after my husband, and He will find him. He has promised us that He will. He has promised that none are lost. We just have to work hard to not have that fear. Many of our problems come from fear. A lot of what we do and how we respond is based in fear, but really, we just need to let go and realize that Heavenly Father is in charge. I have to let go and trust in Heavenly Father, and trust that His mercy and His justice will work according to His timetable, not mine and not anyone else's.

I absolutely have no idea about the future of my marriage. My journey really must be taken one day at a time. I also know that everything is contingent upon agency. I have no control over how my husband uses his agency. I am willing to work on our marriage. I am willing to go through a recovery process. I have no agency or choice over where he chooses to go from here. He could divorce me, or he could be softened and changed. The Lord knows, and that has been one of the hardest things. I truly have to put all of my dreams and expectations for my life and for the life of my family members upon the altar and just give them to Heavenly Father because I just don't know how the future will play out.

I really want to emphasize that just because we lose trust with our spouse doesn't mean we have to lose trust with the Lord. We might be so overwhelmed at first that we lose faith and trust and become caught up in despair. I just think that it is really important that we move out of that place and turn to the Lord. He knows our trials. He knows our pain.

HOPE AND HEALING IN SHIRLEY'S LIFE

Shirley recognized, as did many of the women we interviewed, that trusting her husband may or may not become a reality, but she did learn to put her trust in God. The emotions women feel in reaction to their husbands' addictions can bring them to their knees pleading with Heavenly Father to help them feel His abiding love. As Shirley prayed, she felt the tremendous love of her Heavenly Father. This reminded her that she was a cherished daughter of God, and the process of restoring her identity and self-worth was underway. As women turn to their Heavenly Father during these trying times, they too can come to feel their Father's love. They too can learn to place their trust in Him, in His timetable, and in His justice and mercy. Women can also turn to their Savior and rely upon His grace and mercy, for a loving Father has placed Him at the very center of hope, healing, and happiness. Elder Jeffrey R. Holland said, "The central fact, the crucial foundation, the chief doctrine, and the greatest expression of divine love in the eternal plan of salvation—truly a 'plan of happiness,' as Alma called it (Alma 42:8)—is the Atonement of the Lord Jesus Christ."[95]

Dr. Skinner told us that it was not easy to help women move forward spiritually when pornography has been part of their marriage. He thought that women need to be reminded of spiritual feelings and impressions from the past, while working to see the love of God in their life. He said:

From my perspective, it is important that I begin by getting to their spiritual roots, "Do you know that there is a God? Do you believe that He cares about you and loves you? What experiences have you had that you know that God has been with you?" I try to reignite things of truth that they already know—feelings, promptings, times where they know that God has led them, helped them, blessed them. Because what happens in trauma is that you stop being objective. You stop being able to see the world around you. You are seeing it from trauma, hurt, pain, lack of trust, rather than seeing from the other corner where there is love, care, and validation from a loving God.

We also have to separate humanness, the arm of flesh, from the power of God, the love of God, the healing of God, the caring and compassion of God. It is important that women don't forget that He is loving, that He is lamenting and suffering because of what they are suffering. We have to separate God from humanness because when you put your trust in the arm of flesh you will always be let down. I'm not saying that everyone is always going to let you down, but as humans we will hurt each other; and we will make mistakes.

Although you may feel your faith is fading as you face the uncertainty of the future, be assured that there is a "balm in Gilead," and healing will eventually be realized. When faith in Jesus Christ is exercised, He will heal and guide. He has promised that He will go before you. He will be on your right hand and on your left, and His Spirit shall be in your heart, and His angels round about you, to bear you up (see D&C 84:88). His promises are sure, and His love is unfailing.

MOVING FORWARD 7

As you keep moving forward, you can stay upright
even when outside forces try to pull you down.
– Bonnie L. Oscarson[96]

At the time of our interviews, some women had moved forward with
their lives. They were triggered, angry, or sad less often. For those who
chose to remain married, it meant accepting the long-term realities of
living with their husband's addiction, even though he might have periods
of sobriety. Perhaps some women will feel the need to have periods of sep-
aration in order to move forward. These women used a variety of ways to
cope, such as women's support groups, individual therapy, exercise (espe-
cially yoga), and being educated about the addiction. Other women were
still in the midst of feeling betrayed and hurt. If these feelings of betrayal
remained unaddressed over many years, women seemed stuck in their
anger and pain. In this chapter, we will talk about ways women might
navigate this painful experience, realize their blessings, and start the pro-
cess of forgiveness. The only sure thing in this journey is the significance
of keeping faith in the Savior and His Atonement. When women keep
Christ central to their lives, they will keep moving forward.

LIVES CENTERED ON CHRIST

Despite the pain and the evil that women saw around them, they felt
strengthened and found purpose and direction when their lives were cen-
tered on the Savior. Elder Richard J. Maynes compared our lives to a piece

of clay upon the potter's wheel—if it is not centered on the wheel, then it will never become what it is supposed to become. He stated the following:

> The world in which we live is similar to the potter's spinning wheel, and the speed of that wheel is increasing. Like the clay on the potter's wheel, we must be centered as well. Our core, the center of our lives, must be Jesus Christ and His gospel. Living a Christ-centered life means we learn about Jesus Christ and His gospel and then we follow His example and keep His commandments with exactness. . . . If our lives are centered in Jesus Christ, He can successfully mold us into who we need to be in order to return to His and Heavenly Father's presence in the celestial kingdom. The joy we experience in this life will be in direct proportion to how well our lives are centered on the teachings, example, and atoning sacrifice of Jesus Christ.[97]

In Bruce C. Hafen's book *Covenant Hearts: Why Marriage Matters and How to Make It Last,* Marie Hafen shared her perspective on the importance of having Christ as the center of our lives:

> We must be vigilant in holding on to the Savior and staying with Him in the center. When Christ is the focus of our lives, we know He will help us if we have the spiritual maturity to stay with Him no matter what is swirling around us.[98]

No matter what type of adversity we are handling or where we are in the healing journey, keeping Christ as the center of our lives is the best way to move forward. It is comforting to know that Isaiah referred to Christ as "a man of sorrows, and acquainted with grief" (Isaiah 53:3).

MOVING FORWARD THROUGH SUFFERING

In an essay on suffering, *New York Times* columnist David Brooks asserts that when people recover from suffering, they come out different; they emerge from the suffering as different people than they were before. Suffering has required they dig deeper into themselves to find out who they really are, which includes a better understanding of their limitations. Further, he thinks that people realize that they are no longer "masters of the situation [that has caused the suffering], but neither are they helpless. They can't determine the course of their pain, but they can participate in responding to it."[99]

We found that many of the women we interviewed emerged as different women. They had endured suffering, but some were able to reflect upon the growth they experienced and the blessings received from a merciful and loving Heavenly Father. Many told us that this experience has helped them realize how strong they really are. Melanie explained it this way: "I have learned that I am a lot stronger than I realized. . . . Going through this and allowing the Lord to share in these strengths with me has been the difference." Claire shared this:

> I have realized that I am a lot stronger than I ever believed I was. I have learned to stand up for myself. I have learned to deal with trial and hardship more calmly and with more grace. I have also learned that I can do hard things. This marriage has been hard, but so far I have done it. I have learned a lot, and I have been able to grow because of his addiction. I have become more confident and even more fun than I ever was.

Liz told us that while experiencing this trial she has not only learned a great deal about the addiction itself, but she has learned a lot about herself and the Atonement. She explains:

> I have learned a lot about the Atonement and the deeper meaning of it in my life and in the life of my husband. I have learned that Satan is real as I have really felt His power over me and my loved ones. I have learned how easy it is for Satan to find a crack in the door and overcome the will power in your life. I have learned that we cannot do this alone and that we truly need to reach out to each other to overcome it.
>
> I have also learned to love more deeply and more completely. I have learned that people aren't perfect. I have learned that repentance and forgiveness aren't easy, but they are possible. I have learned that I am not responsible for the weaknesses of my husband, that I did not cause his addiction, and that I cannot control the addiction. And I have also learned that despite the addiction of my husband, I can find happiness and peace for myself.

Shirley expressed her thoughts this way:

> While this trial has been devastating for me, at the same time I am really starting to appreciate it as a blessing. Because of this trial, I have a more in-depth understanding of the Atonement, more so than I have ever had before. It has been humbling, and I find myself a lot less judgmental of others. I have become a lot more merciful myself, and I am gaining greater qualities that I know my Heavenly Father wants me to have.

Another way women emerged as having changed is that the suffering increased their understanding of the role opposition plays in the plan of salvation. For example, Courtney told us that, "The plan is to go through trials that will show us what we need to see, to encourage the positive traits that we need to develop, and to allow God to take our flaws. That's what the plan is." Melanie contemplated how her spirituality has struggled but also how she has been strengthened from the trials she experienced.

> He doesn't allow us to go through trials that we aren't going to benefit from, if we allow that to happen. So my spirituality has struggled, but more than struggled it has been strengthened. I have been able to more fully understand the Atonement even more so than when I was on my mission. I have been able to see it work in my life as the wife of an addict. I have been able to feel my Savior's love more than ever before, and He has been able to remove the pain from my chest. I know the Lord allows us to go through trials because we gain fuller understanding of the good and the bad just like the scriptures tell us. There is definitely opposition in all things, and I have learned to be grateful for that opposition. It has definitely made me much stronger.

Women can acknowledge the difficulty and trauma of this painful journey and at the same time express gratitude for their own growth and the realization of their own strength. Gratitude can be a remedy for the heartache experienced in life. It has the power to elevate spirits, brighten outlooks, and bring us closer to God. President Lorenzo Snow counseled:

> I have thought sometimes that one of the greatest virtues the Latter-day Saints could possess is gratitude to our Heavenly Father for that which He has bestowed upon us and the path over which He has led us. It may be that walking along in that path has not always been of the most pleasant character; but we have afterwards discovered that those circumstances which have been very unpleasant have often proved of the highest advantage to us. We should always be pleased with the circumstances that surround us and that which the Lord requires at our hands.[100]

The journey through suffering is surely difficult, but is one that does not have to be traveled alone. Joseph Smith, who was no stranger to great adversity, taught that if we place our trust and confidence in the power, wisdom, and love of God, He will move us forward through the most adverse of circumstances. Joseph Smith counseled the early saints to "stand fast . . . hold on a little while longer, and the storm of life will be past, and you will be rewarded by that God whose servants you are."[101]

MOVING FORWARD THROUGH FORGIVENESS

Forgiveness is a very sensitive topic for women who have experienced such adversity in their marriage. The pain, suffering, and betrayal were still so raw for many women that the concept of forgiveness was impossible to consider. Most women realized that forgiveness was essential to their own healing and progression, but only a few felt that they had actually forgiven their husband. Many of the women had learned that offering forgiveness before she was ready proved unsuccessful. Women who allowed themselves to acknowledge and experience the full range of emotions in reaction to their husbands' pornography addictions were prepared to start the healing process. When women are able to acknowledge and experience the full range of their emotions, it is helpful to realize that Christ will honor these emotions and even sit with you in your pain and suffering, no matter how long it takes.

Dr. Janis A. Spring has coined a term, cheap forgiveness, to describe when forgiveness is offered too quickly or too easily. When a woman chooses to sidestep her emotional, spiritual, and even physiological injuries brought on by her husband's pornography addiction in the name of forgiveness, she is not being true to the pain and suffering she has experienced. According to Dr. Spring, this type of forgiveness circumvents the injuries and negates any chance of developing a healthy relationship with yourself or your offender.[102] Dr. Spring believes that some may feel internal or external pressure to forgive sooner than they are ready, and to forgive at any cost, due to their moral or religious upbringing or the expectations that come from others. When this occurs one may risk not asking such basic, yet important questions as, "Is this relationship healthy for me right now?" "Should I trust him with my well-being?" "What makes me think he won't hurt me again?"[103] Dr. Spring summarized that:

> Cheap forgiveness is dysfunctional because it creates an illusion of closeness when nothing has been faced or resolved, and the offender has done nothing to earn it. Silencing your anguish and indignation, you fail to acknowledge or appreciate the harm that was done to you.[104]

Some women may find it easy to gravitate toward cheap forgiveness because of perceived immediate advantages. Dr. Spring outlines some of these advantages but then counters them with corresponding disadvantages. One perceived advantage is that offering cheap forgiveness allows one to remain connected to her offender, but in reality, this only extinguishes any opportunity to develop a more intimate bond. Cheap forgiveness may also cause one to feel morally superior to her offender, but this is likely the very thing that will keep them from growing closer. Additionally, women may believe that cheap forgiveness will nudge her offender toward repentance and is actually good for her health, but in reality, cheap forgiveness will likely give your offender the green light to continue his behavior. Forgiving too quickly may only postpone your healing.

Women may also recognize that forgiving their spouses and trusting them are two separate things. Others may struggle to understand the difference between forgiveness and trust, and declare that forgiveness will never occur until trust is reestablished. Because of these complexities and other roadblocks, achieving forgiveness can be an elusive endeavor. Eventually, women need to choose to forgive in order to experience healing, regardless of if their husbands are repentant or not.

Elder Richard G. Scott shared the following counsel about forgiveness:

> You cannot erase what has been done, but you can forgive. (See D&C 64:10.) Forgiveness heals terrible, tragic wounds, for it allows the love of God to purge your heart and mind of the poison of hate. It cleanses your consciousness of the desire for revenge. It makes place for the purifying, healing, restoring love of the Lord.[105]

When one chooses to forgive, the judgment of the offender is turned over to God. He will balance the scales of justice and mercy for women and their husbands. Best-selling author Virginia H. Pearce declared,

> We always have a choice when we are wounded. We can retaliate, attempting to return the pain to the one who inflicted it. We can pass the hurt on to someone else. Or we can metabolize the pain and treat others differently than we've been treated. Christ is the supreme example of taking the pain in and then not passing it on, instead metabolizing it and diffusing it. We mirror God's mercy to us when we forgive another.[106]

Shirley struggled with forgiving her husband because he was unable to prove that he was trustworthy. Over time, she realized that there is a fine balancing act between mercy and justice. She felt that her husband was always leaning toward wanting more mercy. She discovered that true healing and rebuilding trust cannot take place unless there is a healthy balance of justice and mercy for both spouses. Shirley felt that if her husband could not prove to be trustworthy, she would have to turn it over to God.

> What I am realizing is that it comes down to trust. It really is an issue of trust. We want justice because we think it will allow us to recover and move on. I have learned that what happens with my husband on the justice end is up to the Lord and His timetable. The Lord will seek after him and He will find him. He has promised us that He will. He has promised that none are lost. We just have to work hard to not have fear. Fear is that negative emotion that all of our problems evolve from, and a lot of what we do and how we respond is based on fear. We really need to be willing to let go and realize that Heavenly Father is in charge. The first thing you need to do is to let go of your husband and his problems in a healthy way. You can still love him and pray for him, but you have to let go and trust in Heavenly Father. You have to trust that His mercy and His justice will work according to His timetable—not yours and not anyone else's.

FORGIVENESS IS DIFFERENT THAN TRUST

During our interviews, we recognized that those who struggled the most to forgive their husbands were the women who found it difficult to differentiate between forgiveness and trust. Minnie shared that she would not be able to forgive her husband until she could trust him once again. When David would have setbacks in his pornography addiction this was evidence to her that he could not be trusted.

Recognizing that there was a difference between forgiveness and trust, other wives found it easier to forgive than to trust their spouse. Melanie readily forgave Doug; however, she was unable to trust him so easily. She said, "Forgiveness and trust are two different things." Amber also found that forgiveness for her husband came easily because he had forgiven her of so many things, but after he disclosed everything to her, trusting him again became very difficult. She shared the following:

> When we were engaged I gave Luke a pretty long list of things that I had done in my life and had repented of. He brought forward a

very short list and pornography wasn't on it. Once he finally disclosed everything, trust and honesty went out the window. Now that we are in recovery it is so important for him to remember that his actions speak louder than words.

Claire has also been able to forgive her husband, but she no longer trusts him. She explained:

> There is no trust in our marriage. It has been filled with broken promises, lots of lying, and no follow-through. He would always promise to never do it again, and he would promise to get help, but he would never follow through with it. At one point I told him that if he did it again we would have to separate. I then found out that I thought he had gone a whole year without looking at it, but he was totally lying. This was year four of our marriage, and after that, I stopped trusting him altogether. . . . I really have tried, but until he becomes more consistent with what he is doing to overcome this, there really is no hope of reestablishing trust again.

Of all the wives interviewed, Ashley seemed to struggle the most with trust. She and Michael had only been married for thirteen months when he finally disclosed his pornography addiction. The marriage that she thought had been established on trust and honesty, didn't really ever exist. She said that Michael had so many chances to come clean, and if he had done so, the healing process for their marriage could have begun much earlier. At the time of the interview, she didn't know how she would be able to trust him again.

It is confusing for some because it is difficult to forgive if the other person is not repentant or trustworthy. In the case of pornography addiction, establishing trust is primarily up to the husband. He must become trustworthy through sincere repentance, genuine sorrow, and restitution. Marriage counselor and author Steve Arteburn wrote the following in regards to marital reconciliation:

> There must be genuine sorrow on the part of the betrayer. This also is a key to rebuilding trust. Without it, it's like building a brick wall without cement. The goal of rebuilding trust is that at some point there is genuine sorrow on the part of the one who lived the lie, and genuine forgiveness on the part of the one betrayed. Without both of these conditions, the marital reconciliation is going to be very superficial and very unsatisfying to both parties.[107]

However, Dr. Skinner acknowledged that forgiveness is possible to achieve even when the husband is not trustworthy. He shared that when women forgive it doesn't necessarily mean that they reconcile with their husband. He may still be acting out, but women can choose not to hold animosity and anger anymore. Women can feel sorrow and disappointment when their husband succumbs to pornography, but as women stay emotionally centered they realize that they can be okay no matter what their husband is doing. Dr. Skinner then stated,

> I've seen women stay in marriages that I could not believe that they stayed in, but they no longer felt that animosity. They feel that they are supposed to stay, and sometimes they stay for years, or they stay until something happens that ends the marriage. So you never know. Every relationship has its own unique factors that you need to take into account.

Alice really struggled to forgive her husband because he could never prove he was trustworthy. When asked if she would ever be able to fully trust Shawn, she replied:

> Oh man, I sure hope to. At this point I really don't know. . . . I hate how long it takes to rebuild trust. I wish there was a switch that I could just turn on and it would be there. I want to trust my husband; I want to so badly. There is nothing to be gained from a marriage where there is no trust. . . . It just really takes time so I am watching and waiting, but he has repeatedly hurt me.

It was evident in our interviews that some of the husbands were doing all within their power to rebuild trust in their marriages. Dr. Donald L. Hilton Jr. recommends that husbands do the following in order to restore trust in their marriage:

1. A clean confession followed by complete *appropriate* transparency for the rest of his life.
2. A full commitment to recovery, which includes ecclesiastical and therapeutic support, and 12-step group support.
3. A visible change in attitude, with humility, gratitude, and self-esteem replacing shame, guilt, and pride.[108]

MISTAKEN ASSUMPTIONS ABOUT FORGIVENESS

Another hurdle many women faced in their forgiveness journey was the presence of mistaken assumptions surrounding the concept of forgiveness. Some of these assumptions include:

- I can't enter into the process of forgiving until I feel perfectly safe, comfortable, and ready.

When a woman chooses this route, forgiveness will likely never be realized. Forgiveness is a delicate dance. For some couples, this dance looks something like this: the husband works to make amends, and the wife opens herself up to him and does not allow her doubts and anxieties to play out with each interaction.[109] This requires vulnerability from both husband and wife.

- Forgiveness happens immediately.

This is most likely never the case. Therefore, at what point does forgiveness actually take place? As stated before, forgiveness occurs at different times for different people, and in different ways. It is typically a gradual process that unfolds in stages as time is taken for emotions to catch up to the decision to forgive.[110]

- Once I forgive my husband, all negative feelings toward him will be replaced by positive ones.

Women have suffered deep, emotional injuries that cannot be magically reversed. The brain's ability to reexperience traumatic moments with the same detail and emotional upheaval can strike at any time, even years from now when something triggers a memory. Accepting this as part of the forgiveness process will allow you to make room for negative spikes in emotion, and also allow other positive and tender emotions to coexist, such as sadness, grief, and compassion. Dr. Spring warns women to be prepared: "Forgiving won't wash away the injury; you may be left with a residue of bad feelings and an overwhelming sense of loss."[111] When you forgive, you don't flip a convenient switch and all is healed and forgotten. There will still be grief, anger, and resentment, but these do not have to cancel out any gratitude you have for your husband's genuine acts of contrition, or preempt your own feelings of forgiveness.[112]

- Forgiving my husband would be the same as admitting that my anger toward him was exaggerated or unjustified.

Feeling anger is a healthy, adaptive response to the pain and suffering that results from a spouse's pornography addiction. One woman's angry response will definitely look different than another's. There is no right or wrong to its display. Granting forgiveness does not downplay or discount anger in any situation, and even forgiving your spouse doesn't mean your anger isn't justified. In fact, acknowledging the pain and anger allows you to address it instead of dismiss it. Without this acknowledgement, there is nothing to forgive. It is possible to forgive and still stand by the recognition that your husband has crossed the line and must be held accountable.[113]

- When I forgive my husband, I in turn make myself weak and vulnerable. I'm better off denying my pain in order to make peace.

There is no truth in either statement. In fact, the exact opposite is true. Dr. Spring states:

> Genuine forgiveness takes strength and resolve. By standing up for yourself, you insist that you've been wronged and require an accounting in the *ledger of justice*. You don't give up your position of power; you give up your preoccupation with power. You don't dismiss your need for restitution; you let him work with you to achieve restitution.[114]

FORGIVENESS MEANS RECONCILIATION

By linking forgiveness with reconciliation, women may become reluctant to offer forgiveness to their husbands. The processes of forgiveness and reconciliation must be considered separately. Women can choose to forgive but not to reconcile. This may help women stay in an emotionally safe place. Reconciliation may depend on a husband's trustworthiness.[115]

By dispelling these false assumptions and realizing that forgiveness and trust are two different things, the "delicate dance" of forgiveness can begin. Dr. Skinner believes that forgiveness becomes somewhat of a dance. He states:

> You cannot cookie cut the forgiveness process. This is a process that takes time and energy, and both parties are affected. They have to learn how to be forgiving and to be forgiven. The person that has done the offending has to learn how to forgive himself, as well as earn forgiveness from the people they have offended.

The delicate dance of forgiveness involves three different steps: forgiving yourself, forgiving your husband, and allowing the Atonement of Jesus Christ to help you with both.

FORGIVING YOURSELF

The step of forgiving yourself may be somewhat confusing when it is your husband's pornography addiction that has led to your pain and suffering. But when life hands over something this challenging and heart-wrenching, it is likely to bring out the worst in any wife. Under these circumstances, myriad feelings and emotions rise to the surface, and perhaps reveal a side to you that you never knew existed. Some of the wives we interviewed admitted that this was the case for them. They displayed their feelings and emotions outwardly by screaming at their husbands, throwing dishes, breaking things, saying things they weren't proud of, and even punching holes in the walls. Others internalized their feelings and emotions, shut down, and even blamed themselves for the addiction and other problems in their marriage. In either case, many of the wives felt guilt and shame for the way they responded but realized that until they could forgive themselves, moving forward would be difficult.

Dr. Skinner shared this insight:

> The person who has been offended has to look at their own hurt and their own beliefs, and sometimes their own behaviors, which have in some ways contributed to the negative outcome. For example, if I am always difficult; if I am always yelling and screaming because I am hurt; if my behaviors in those moments, although natural and normal, are unbecoming, or if I have said things that are cutting and harsh, those are things that I have to look at and say that those are things that I don't want to be. This allows you to redefine yourself in the process of forgiving [yourself].

When a wife is able to replace self-blame with personal accountability and recognize the need to forgive herself, she is not only redefining herself in the process, she is refining herself and she is also opening the doors to healing. Elder Boyd K. Packer explained the importance of forgiving yourself in order to heal: "Forgiveness is powerful spiritual medicine. To extend forgiveness, that soothing balm, to those who have offended you is to heal. And, more difficult yet, when the need is there, forgive yourself!"[116]

President Dieter F. Uchtdorf expressed the following:

> When the Lord requires that we forgive all men, that includes for-giving ourselves. Sometimes, of all the people in the world, the one who is the hardest to forgive—as well as perhaps the one who is most in need of our forgiveness—is the person looking back at us in the mirror.[117]

Forgiving yourself and others is a miracle that takes place in the heart, and is enabled through the Atonement of Jesus Christ. By accept-ing this gift, you can be at peace, knowing that we too are human and the Lord loves and understands us. Forgiveness of self and others unlocks a closed and accusing heart and allows the healing journey to begin. Being merciful with yourself opens the door of the heart and allows you to show mercy to yourself.

FORGIVING YOUR HUSBAND

When men have brought pornography and all of its devastating effects into marriage, women will likely need to eventually forgive him for many things. Women might need to forgive their husbands for the deep sense of betrayal and for his lack of honesty. They might need to forgive him for the poor example he has set for their children, for breaking sacred covenants, and for not being emotionally available. Or, they might need to forgive him for viewing pornography in the first place and allowing it to become an addiction. Whatever a husband's offenses might be, forgive-ness is for the wife's peace and well-being.

Dr. Spring notes that when women are able to offer genuine forgive-ness, they begin to see their offender in a more benevolent and objective light. Dr. Spring warns that when you refuse to forgive, it can dimin-ish any hope of recovering the relationship because women will continue to define her husband in terms of how he has harmed her and dismiss any other information that might rehabilitate him in her eyes. Women can spend so much time hating their offender and justifying their anger toward him that they may not notice or appreciate the beneficial roles he has played in their life.[118] At this point bitterness and resentment are held so tightly that any type of reconciliation becomes impossible. In other words, by not allowing forgiveness at the right time, women also run the risk of further damaging an already broken relationship.

There is a chance, however, that an offender may never be repentant or emotionally available. At this point, is forgiveness possible? Dr. Spring declares that the blessings of genuine forgiveness can still be realized but additional steps will need to be taken. It is here where women must make the choice to take control of their pain, explore the depths of their injury, and fashion a working relationship with their offender. Although women are not responsible for the harm that was done, they can accept the responsibility of recovery and begin to discover how to survive and rise above the injury.[119] Women can decide how they are going to live the rest of their lives, and forgiveness empowers them to make peace with the past, which is a courageous and life-affirming approach.

During our interviews, we discovered that some of the husbands were repentant and remorseful, while others were still in denial, ignoring the extent of their addiction and the trauma it was causing. However, there seemed to be one thing that helped women more easily accept and forgive their husband. Several of the women shared how their husbands were exposed to pornography when they were children and had been addicted ever since. This caused the women to consider their own children and how they would feel if this happened to one of them. Courtney talked about how heartbreaking this would be for her and how she would do everything within her power to love and help her child. As she considered this, she realized that she needed to view her husband in this same light. Some of the wives also shared that their husbands had a lot of emotional baggage from their dysfunctional childhoods, and that they had turned to pornography to help them deal with the pain and stressors in their life. Pornography in this case became their husband's drug of choice. Sterling Ellsworth, PhD, explains this concept:

> Children need love like fish need water. If they don't get the real thing [at home or in other relationships during childhood] they reach for love substitutes such as food, sexual gratification, and pornography. . . . When true love is given to a child, he grows up sensitive to his own identity. . . . He doesn't need to go looking for love because his love bucket is full.[120]

President Spencer W. Kimball taught this same concept: "Jesus saw sin as wrong but also was able to see sin as springing from deep and unmet needs on the part of the sinner. This permitted him to condemn the sin without condemning the individual. . . . We need to be able to look deeply enough into the lives of others to see the basic causes for their failures and shortcomings."[121] By understanding where your husband's addiction springs from, your pain and suffering may be lightened, you will have a desire to extend mercy, and forgiveness will ensue.

Elder Bruce C. Hafen shared the reminder that we marry the person's past as well as his present:

> You don't just marry a person in the present—you marry that person's past. And often the past will control the present in ways a partner could never understand without knowing the past. We must refrain from judging the present until we have a better sense of what it means in the light of the past, as hard as that may be to uncover.[122]

When a wife is able to hold her husband accountable for his choices, but at the same time look upon him with compassion and an understanding of his past, forgiveness can be achieved in its own time and in its own way.

ACHIEVING FORGIVENESS THROUGH THE ATONEMENT

It is ultimately through the Atonement of Jesus Christ that forgiving others will be made possible. You will begin to recognize that your husband's behavior is about him—his innate disposition, the traumatic experiences of his past, and his responses to the stressors of life. Being able to step back and clearly view your husband through this lens allows you to see him wrestle with his own demons, and perhaps for the first time come to understand how much hurt and shame he has experienced. President Dieter F. Uchtdorf offered the following counsel:

> The pure love of Christ can remove the scales of resentment and wrath from our eyes, allowing us to see others the way our Heavenly Father sees us: as flawed and imperfect mortals who have potential and worth far beyond our capacity to imagine. Because God loves us so much, we too must love and forgive each other.[123]

Dr. Skinner shared with us that when he sees couples who apply the Atonement to work through the problems pornography has created in their marriage, it is absolutely beautiful to watch. They learn how to forgive and to see the hand of God in their life. He also commented how heartbreaking it is when marriages don't survive the devastating effects of pornography. However, peace and forgiveness are still possible through the Atonement of Jesus Christ, and no blessings will be denied. Elder Dallin H. Oaks shared similar counsel:

> Personal circumstances vary greatly. We cannot control and we are not responsible for the choices of others, even when they impact us so painfully. I am sure the Lord loves and blesses husbands and wives who lovingly try to help spouses struggling with such deep problems as pornography or other addictive behavior or with the long-term consequences of childhood abuse.
>
> Whatever the outcome and no matter how difficult your experiences, you have the promise that you will not be denied the blessings of eternal family relationships if you love the Lord, keep His commandments, and just do the best you can. When young Jacob "suffered afflictions and much sorrow" from the actions of other family members, Father Lehi assured him, "Thou knowest the greatness of God; and he shall consecrate thine afflictions for thy gain" (2 Nephi 2:1–2). Similarly, the Apostle Paul assured us that "all things work together for good to them that love God" (Romans 8:28).[124]

In the following section, we share Liz's story. Her story is one of heartache, depression, loneliness, and betrayal, but is also a story of faith, persistence, love, forgiveness, and hope. She recounts the incredible stressors her husband's addiction placed upon her and how it was a very tumultuous time for her and her family. She also shares the recognizable blessings that followed, as well as her newfound hope for happiness and her husband's sobriety. Liz exemplifies a woman who has emerged different as a result of her suffering.

LIZ'S STORY

My husband, Nathan, and I have been married nineteen years. About seven years ago, I discovered his pornography use. He admitted that he had been exposed as a teenager yet was able to stay worthy and serve a mission. Pornography was not a big problem for him until seven years ago, when he was working on his master's degree as well as working full-time. During this time, he turned to pornography as a relief from work and school stresses. In addition to working long hours at the office, he came home and worked on schoolwork long hours at night. I knew things weren't right, and the long hours of studying turned into super late nights staying at work on the computer until early hours of the morning.

I confronted him one night about the late nights. He finally admitted his addiction to pornography and his loss of control.

The initial discovery was really hard on me. I had followed Nathan several states away from my family in order for him to follow his dream to finish his master's degree and change careers. Because we lived away from family, the discovery stayed a secret from everyone except for me. My husband worked with his bishop over the period of a couple years and it felt like he was trying to work things out. But he never sought counseling, which bothered me.

We only had one joint meeting with the bishop. The bishop told me that I needed to step out of all my extracurricular activities outside the home and devote all my efforts to Nathan and strengthening my marriage. I did as he asked, but it bothered me that I was asked to do one more thing. I was already taking care of the house, yard, garden, kids, finances, supporting him while he worked and studied. I had to give one more thing? I really felt like I was being blamed for the problem. But I followed the counsel of my bishop and did as I was asked. I quit volunteering in the schools and working with the Scouts. It was tough and it led to some depression for me.

There were many periods of abstinence and relapse. Some times were easier to forgive than others. I rarely lost my temper, as it did no good and just made Nathan stay away from me longer. Usually I gave him the silent treatment until I could talk about it without losing control. There were days we couldn't even talk about anything, because everything was so wrapped up in the addiction.

For years, I didn't know how to handle Nathan's acting out and his obsession with pornography. I stalked his online use, asked pointed questions about where he was and what he was doing, made him feel guilty, and gave him ultimatums that he had to choose between his addiction and his family. Sometimes I even went to his work late at night when I knew he was in his office viewing pornography. I honked my car horn until he came out. Not the best method, but it sometimes worked.

After looking at pornography, I felt my husband always wanted more from me. He wanted to do more experimenting sexually and wanted me to be skinnier and prettier. I felt like he wanted me to be more like what he was viewing. Thinking like that really crushed my self-esteem for years. I was extremely angry and didn't understand why the pull to pornography was so strong. But I deeply love my husband and I always have, so I easily forgave him because I couldn't picture life without him as part of it. The hardest part to forgive was when my husband was actively seeking companionship from other ladies and I stumbled on his e-mails to them. I wasn't sure if I would ever be able to trust him again.

The following year after Nathan's initial disclosure, I got pregnant. Then I had a late-term miscarriage, which was really rough. The miscarriage deepened my depression and further alienated me from my husband, which only deepened his pornography addiction. He turned to pornography not knowing where to find relief from what he felt were my problems. This was one of my lowest points. At this point, the pornography use had become more hard-core. I knew we were in trouble. We pretty much stayed together because of our five kids.

The following year, we got pregnant again. It was a high-risk pregnancy, and I was put on bed rest. His pornography use increased again. Because of the severity of what he was viewing and doing, a Church disciplinary council was convened and Nathan was released from his position of leadership in the Church. Knowing about what my husband did that led to a Church disciplinary council pushed me over the edge emotionally.

I felt totally betrayed, worthless, ugly, depressed, and my self-esteem plummeted. I knew my husband really didn't want me or the baby that was soon to be born. Here I was, ready to have our sixth child, and I was ready to walk out of a marriage that we had been in for sixteen years. Neither my husband nor I wanted to stay, but still, we both stayed for our kids.

We were miserable. Our communication was almost nonexistent. Life was tense and unhappy. I lapsed into a deep depression, as did Nathan. I spent a good deal of time crying in bed, lost in the world that I didn't know what to do with.

The closest LDS marriage counselor was three hours away one way. We made the trip once, and decided that it wasn't worth the six hours in a car for a forty-five-minute visit.

Nathan wasn't able to participate in Church activity, so my dad came and blessed our baby and baptized our eight-year-old. The blessing that came out of that is that I finally had to tell my parents what was going on in our marriage. I finally had support from them. Before that time, the only people that knew were the Church leaders that had participated in the disciplinary council. It was really difficult on my husband for my family to know. His family never did and still doesn't know. These events set him in motion and he started working toward making things right. But it was an extremely difficult time for me.

The loneliness I felt led to deeper, almost debilitating depression for me. However, after some time it also led me to take action for myself. I started to research and look for anything and everything that could help me and my husband. I read numerous books, articles, watched videos put out by therapists, and pored over the *Ensign* and scriptures. Being so far from counseling was a real detriment to me, and I think hindered my recovery. If I could go back, I would find a way to go to a therapist, even if it wasn't an LDS one. I was so lost and I had no one to talk to.

The very best thing that I found was a phone-in 12-step program for families of addicts. That group became my literal lifeline. I counted the hours until I could call in and receive strength from them. I loved the group. I really read and studied the material all week so I would be spiritually ready to meet with them. They saved me and gave me the strength to save my marriage.

I participated in the 12-step group for more than two years. I would recommend it to every spouse faced with a similar situation. It was that powerful for me. When I learned that I wasn't responsible for his addiction and that it was beyond my control, I started taking care of myself. I worked the steps. I focused on my own needs and my own weaknesses. I didn't ignore my husband's addiction, but I didn't let it take control of me either. When I started taking care of my own needs and not being controlled by the addiction, I began to get my life back.

During the lowest of the low, Nathan lost his job of seven years. While they didn't state his computer use as the cause of his termination, I think it played a big factor. As he couldn't concentrate at work, he was always on the computer doing other things. He was hired at another company at which he worked for eight months. During this time of great stress with changes in employment, I think my husband was humbled to realize that this addiction had almost taken everything he had—his job, his home, and his family.

We started working as a couple to pull our family together. Slowly my husband and I found some common ground. We both started attending separate phone-in 12-step groups. We read marriage and pornography literature and discussed them together. A new leader moved into our branch that understood Nathan's challenges, and finally there was someone to help Nathan get through the steps that he needed to take. That leader also supported my children and me. For the first time in several years, we felt wanted and loved. It made a huge difference in our spirituality and our wanting to come back into the Church and get our family put back together.

My husband lost another job and we were unemployed for about six months. This time was horribly stressful. However, we continued to work together, and were able to help and strengthen each other. Nathan was finally in full fellowship in the Church. He was once again in a leadership position and it was actually a good thing for my older teenage boys to watch this transformation through the repentance process.

I came to the point where I had to forgive Nathan and move on. Forgiving him has made our marriage stronger because he knows that I will stand by him and won't leave him to fight alone. He knows that we are a team. We talked a lot as a family about choices and consequences. We talked about loving each other despite what we do, while not condoning the actions. We talked about pornography and the power of this terrible addiction. It actually was a balm that started healing each of us, and it made us stronger as a family unit.

Four months ago, my husband got a job in Arizona. We relocated our family here and got a fresh new start. It has been wonderful to have LDS resources at our fingertips and for us to have a supportive Church unit that knows us and loves us, without all the gossip and the speculations. Our family is starting to heal. Trust issues between Nathan and me still come up and our intimacy still struggles. I have hope that someday things will be okay. There is still a journey ahead. But I am finally free from depression and I have the support of wonderful family and friends here in Arizona. I am hopeful that we can find happiness and sobriety from addiction in the future.

LIZ'S STORY AND MOVING FORWARD

Liz's story of being a loving and supportive wife was a familiar one. She truly loved her husband and wanted to do all within her power to help him with his addiction. She, like so many others, had to take the long, painful journey of discovering that despite her love and righteous desires, she could not control her husband's addiction, nor was she responsible for it. She suffered the same symptoms of betrayal, feelings of worthlessness, and deepening depression as do so many other wives whose husbands struggle with a pornography addiction. Liz's story serves as a powerful example of faith, persistence, forgiveness, and love, and the blessings that come in unexpected ways. It inspires hope for those who are still struggling. We recognize that although the journey is long and painful, and undoubtedly there will still be struggles ahead, there will be fresh starts, healing, happiness, and even sobriety.

EPILOGUE

And then the day came when the risk to remain tight, in a bud, became more painful than the risk it took to blossom.

– Elizabeth Appell[125]

It has been almost three years since we interviewed women to hear their stories of love, betrayal, pain, hope, and healing. When we first interviewed these women, many were full of feelings of love and hope for their husbands but also feelings of betrayal, fear, and concern about their futures. They worried if their husbands would find and stay on the path of recovery. Just before this book was to be published, we caught up with some of the women to see how their lives have played out. Again, we were humbled by each woman's willingness to share her experiences living with pornography in her marriage. We were amazed at the personal strength each woman displayed as she faced life's challenges and were also encouraged by the deep understanding each had gained about Christ's love and His Atonement. We talked with Sarah (chapter 1), Alice (chapter 2), Ashley (chapter 3), Courtney (chapter 4), Cynthia (chapter 5), Shirley (chapter 6), Liz (chapter 7), and Melanie (throughout the chapters). Each woman was asked what had occurred in her life since our interview and factors she thought had contributed to where she was emotionally and spiritually. In addition, we asked what advice she would give to others reading this book.

Since the time of our first interview, there were many changes in their lives and circumstances. Some had moved from where they lived at the time of our first interview, and others had purchased new homes. Of the eight women that we re-interviewed, two had divorced (Ashley and Shirley) while the others remained married. Some women told us about pregnancies, miscarriages, or new babies that had been born. Courtney was now living with chronic, unexplained health problems in addition to Randy's pornography addiction.

During the initial interviews, we found that each woman's healing journey was unique. In these second interviews, we likewise discovered that each woman continued to employ her own unique strengths as she persisted through the process of healing and moving forward, in whatever form moving forward took for her. Many continued to emphasize that there is no one right way to heal and move forward through this challenge. Each woman's approach to recovery and her life's circumstances remained consistent with the approach she had originally taken at the time of our first interview.

TIME HAD CHANGED THEM

One similarity we observed across interviews was that while *women had not forgotten the pain they were experiencing at the time of the initial interview, for many, their pain had decreased.* It wasn't merely the passage of time that had lessened their pain; rather the women had worked hard on their own recovery, including acknowledging and living with their emotions, moving ahead with their lives, and relying on the Savior's Atonement. Sarah shared that overall, she felt she had become a *healthier* version of herself.

The passage of time allowed women to have greater distance between the hard stuff that was going on at the time of our initial interview. Cynthia found hope in moving forward because she could see how things were not as difficult as they had been in the past. One of the reasons the pain had lessened was that the women had worked extremely hard to see the positive changes in their lives. They were intentional about their healing and had made it a priority.

PERSONAL GROWTH

Another similarity was that *women saw tremendous personal growth in themselves, and if they had remained married, in their spouse and marriage.* Women felt that their personal growth came as they worked on their own recovery, reached out to share their experiences with others, and relied on the Savior's Atonement. Shelby said developing a stronger relationship with her Heavenly Father and her Savior, accepting Their unconditional love, and striving to become as They see her, has helped her grow. Trusting and having faith in God were vital to the personal growth many women experienced.

Women who remained married told us that if their husbands had been working on their recoveries, they had seen notable progress in their husbands and their relationships with them. Generally, husbands had increased in their self-awareness, were more gentle and patient, and had become better at communicating with their wives. Courtney told us of a remarkable transformation in her marriage. Because of her undiagnosed health condition where she frequently faints and has seizures, she can't control her body, can't be alone, and can't take care of her new baby by herself. She feels completely out of control in every aspect of her life, and Randy has really had to step it up. He still attends 12-step meetings and therapy, but has not experienced long-term sobriety from the pornography addiction. However, she said that he has become a source of emotional and psychological safety, a safe-haven for her. As you recall from the introduction chapter, this is the quintessential definition of a secure attachment in marriage. Courtney stated:

> Trust between us has changed. He has learned to say, "I know I've behaved that way in the past and you have every right to feel that way now." He sees it and he sees me. He has set aside his need to protect himself. I feel like he's seen me at my worst and at my best. I've seen him become more gentle and tender, and we've become better at seeing the best in each other.

HEALING IS POSSIBLE

Another theme that we heard from women was that *healing is possible with or without their spouse, whether they remained married or not.* Melanie told us that when Christ was on the earth, He worked with individuals and focused on the one, on an individual's personalized healing. The Savior knows of our pain and suffering, and He is always there for each one of us. Like the good Samaritan, when Christ finds us wounded at the wayside, He will bind up our wounds and care for us (see Luke 10:34).

Additionally, Sarah emphasized that it is crucial for women to understand that it is more important to focus on their own healing rather than developing an unhealthy dependency or focusing exclusively on healing the marriage. Individuals need to work on their own recovery before they can begin to work on healing their marriage. In order to ensure their own healing, several women told us that they continued to attend 12-step meetings, worked on overcoming their own "triggers," and were able to generate hope by getting outside of themselves. Shelby shared that service is the best way for her to heal. President Dieter F. Uchtdorf taught:

> As we extend our hands and hearts toward others in Christlike love, something wonderful happens to us. Our own spirits become healed, more refined, and stronger. We become happier, more peaceful, and more receptive to the whisperings of the Holy Spirit.[126]

Sarah shared a rewarding experience that occurred since we last interviewed her. Hank was serving as the elders quorum president when he received a call that a sister needed a blessing because her husband was unavailable to give her one. Hank was unable to find a companion to go with him, so he took Sarah. As they visited with the sister, they learned that her husband had a pornography addiction and that he had relapsed, and the sister was quite distressed by the relapse. It was very meaningful for Sarah to listen to Hank give a blessing to the sister, a blessing that she wished someone had given her when she first found out about Hank's addiction. This was one of many experiences that has helped Sarah heal.

One regret Cynthia has is that she didn't reach out for help sooner to jump-start the healing process, especially because she knew help was available. She isolated herself and suffered the pain alone for the first two months after learning of her husband's addiction and affair. She finally found the courage to seek help online. It took an entire year before she allowed herself to seek in-person help.

We also learned from these follow-up interviews that being honest with one another was essential for the marriage to heal. Alice told us that her husband's openness and honesty do not necessarily mean he has obtained total sobriety. But honesty is essential to the healing process. Alice felt that after she had the emotional space to heal, one of the major contributing factors to her healing process was that Shawn could be completely honest with her about his recovery. It is interesting to note that some people believe that honesty is the highest form of intimacy. Pornography disrupts and even destroys every form of intimacy, but when a man can be completely honest about his addiction and his recovery, and a woman can be completely honest about her feelings and how her husband's pornography addiction has affected her, all forms of intimacy can be resurrected over time.

BEING OPEN WITH OTHERS

For many women, *being open with others about the pornography addiction has allowed them to heal.* In a variety of ways, women shared how they have been able to be more open with others about how they have lived with the addiction in their marriage. Oftentimes, these women have become the go-to person in their ward or network of friends when someone discovers her husband has a pornography addiction. Sarah told us that recovery consumed their lives in a positive way after their mutual decision to be open about it with others. Sarah shared their addiction story in sacrament meeting, and Hank, who was serving as elders quorum president, was also able to share his own struggles with members of his quorum. This opened the door for others to feel comfortable sharing their struggles, and a weight was lifted for Sarah and Hank, as they no longer had to bear this burden alone. Liz has also discovered the healing that takes place by reaching out to others who have experienced a pornography addiction in their marriage. She finds it very healing to talk about it. She has met multiple women on Facebook who she has been able to help by offering support and sharing her own experiences. One of the things Ashley has found to be healing is speaking about her experiences at firesides and youth gatherings. Cynthia finds it therapeutic to offer help to those who are suffering from similar circumstances. She has discovered a different level of healing that takes place when she compassionately reaches out to others, as the Savior did, to succor them in their afflictions (see Alma 7:12). Serving those who deal with a spouse's addiction has helped her come to know her Savior better, and it is her hope that she has helped others do the same.

The words of an unfamiliar song illustrate her thoughts and feelings:

> You took my hand, helped me understand
> The daughter I was meant to be.
> I chose the right as I followed your light—
> Knowing He was right by your side.
> And when the path seemed too hard, and the road grew dark
> It was you who ransomed me.

You bade me to come and partake of His love,
And now I'm beginning to see:

Because of you I know my Savior;
Because of you I feel His love.
In all you do, I see my Savior.
I know you were sent from above.[127]

As women reached out for help and offered their help to others, they served as a light to one another. Both the giver and the receiver were comforted and edified as they journeyed together (see D&C 50:22, 1 Thessalonians 5:11).

FORGIVENESS AND HEALING

Women also learned a great deal about forgiveness and healing. A few women told us that forgiveness came about early and easily for them but that healing took much longer. Many women realized that being able to forgive is truly a miracle made possible through the Atonement of Jesus Christ. Cynthia told us that it is a miracle to be able remove herself from her husband's repentance process and to understand that it is his own process of healing and obtaining forgiveness from Jesus Christ. She told us that she has found great peace in recognizing that she cannot control his healing or his repentance—it is between him and the Lord. Liz also learned to allow her husband to be fully accountable for his actions and to accept that she is not responsible for extending judgment or mercy or for his own healing and recovery. Once she was able to turn everything completely over to the Lord, she found peace.

Cynthia reminded us that when her husband initially disclosed the one-night affair and pornography use, she offered him immediate forgiveness. But she eventually learned that forgiveness and healing are two different things. She used the analogy of being hit by a truck to explain the difference between the two. She said:

> For me, it is easy to offer forgiveness to someone who might have just hit you with a truck. But you still have broken bones and wounds that will need to heal. I discovered that it is okay for me to be angry with my husband and to even hate him at times for the wounds he inflicted on me. I have found that it is important to acknowledge those feelings and process them in a healthy manner, but that doesn't mean I haven't forgiven him. Even though forgiveness is a necessary part of healing, it is still different from healing.

Liz also emphasized that forgiveness involves allowing yourself to experience all the emotions that you feel, inviting Christ to sit with you in those emotions, and then when you are ready, processing those feelings in a healthy manner and then turning them over to the Savior.

NO GUARANTEES IN LIFE

Many women have become more accepting of the fact that life, including their husbands' addictions and the futures of their marriages, is more tenuous, and that there are no guarantees that life will work out in the way they want or have planned. A few women acknowledged that the future is unknown and that there are no guarantees that their husbands will stay sober or that their marriages will succeed. At the same time, women recognize that if their husbands do relapse, they will be starting at a different and an even healthier place than they were in at the time of the initial interview because of their own and their spouses' recovery work over the past several years. Both husband and wife have had to work separately on healing and recovery, but eventually many of these women have learned that there is great power in a strong partnership; true partners can achieve more together than the sum of each working alone. Once husband and wife find healing for themselves, they can then come together and work on strengthening their marriage.[128]

DIFFICULT DECISIONS

Other women had to accept the reality that their husbands were not willing to seek the road to recovery, and this left them with a most difficult choice to make. Do they stay in the marriages, hoping and praying that someday their spouses will seek help and work on recovery? Or do they recognize the unhealthy situations they are in, that things will likely not change anytime soon, and choose to end their marriages? Surely this is something a woman cannot decide on her own. Much prayer and fasting, along with enlisting help from others, such as priesthood leaders, family members, trusted friends, and therapists, is crucial at this juncture. Only the Lord knows the future. The prophet Jacob taught, "For he knoweth all things, and there is not anything save he knows it" (2 Nephi 9:20). The Lord also knows our thoughts and the intents of our hearts (see Alma 8:32), and He sees into the innermost parts of our eternal spirits. The Savior taught, "I know the things that come into your mind, every one of them" (Ezekiel 11:5).

When Ashley was faced with the difficult decision concerning divorce, she prayed fervently to the Lord to know what she should do. She continued reaching out to family members (particularly her mother), friends, and her therapist. The answers didn't come all at once, but eventually she was convinced of what she must do. She shared the following:

> I came to the decision to divorce once I realized that Michael was not serious about recovery. For six weeks, he lied to me about attending counseling sessions with a therapist and visiting with the bishop on a regular basis. I found out about this when the bishop invited us both in for a visit to check our progress. During our visit, he counseled Michael to put me first in his life and to really go overboard in making sure my needs were met every day. As we were leaving, the bishop asked Michael why he hadn't been keeping his appointments to meet with him. I became physically ill as I came to realize Michael had been lying to me this entire time. To make matters worse, Michael came undone on the drive home—stating that the bishop was out of line with his counsel of putting me first and of weekly visits with him. I knew right then it was over. I knew I would never be put first in his life. The women he was viewing were first in his life. He certainly didn't take his stress out on them. We separated at this point and two months later we were divorced.

Shirley's twenty-five-year marriage also ended in divorce. She told us that what ultimately led to the divorce was that her husband's pornography addiction had destroyed any love or natural affection that had previously existed in their marriage. Shirley stated:

> I initially wanted to try and work things out but soon realized that my husband was not willing to try at all. He was still so emotionally and psychologically abusive, so I found it necessary to reflect on my own self-worth and how this relationship was affecting me. I became determined to not allow him to define who I was. I knew the truth about our situation, and I knew it was best to just let go. I could not control his addiction, and I could not control the outcome of his recovery. Through much prayer and fasting, I came to know my Heavenly Father did not want me to remain in an abusive situation, so I got out.

Elder Neal A. Maxwell once stated, "The winds of tribulation, which blow out some men's candles of commitment, only fan the fires of faith of [others]."[129] Although Shirley and Ashley's husbands had their candles of commitment blown out, their own fires of faith were fanned. Ashley shared:

> I have found a greater faith in myself, in the Atonement, and in the Savior's love and His gospel. I now only focus on things that bring me joy such as running, hiking, exercising, the outdoors, and family and friends.

Shirley states that she is very happy to be where she is right now. She has cut all emotional ties with her husband and focuses her energy on herself and her children. She is working hard on her own recovery, developing new hobbies and talents, and allowing a whole new world of opportunities to open up to her. She has more trust and faith in God and knows that everything will be okay. She recognizes that miracles do happen daily. She also realizes that she is never alone—the Savior has never left her side, and she is going to keep moving forward in a positive direction.

In conclusion, each woman worked on her recovery in distinctive and unique ways, depending on many factors such as her willingness to reach out to others, social support, family situation, personality, and connection to Heavenly Father and the Savior. While not all of the women were completely healed, the women we re-interviewed were moving forward with their lives and families with hope and positive attitudes. For women who remained married, they felt their marriages had improved, primarily because they worked on their own recovery first and learned that only their husband could work on his recovery. For women who had divorced, they believed that they had been able to move forward with a strong and confident determination to remain close to Heavenly Father and the Savior. While none of the women felt they would seek out this trial, they were grateful for the learning and growth they had experienced. These women had truly lived in the refiner's fire, but they emerged polished and eager to progress in their mortal journey.

NO MORE HOPELESS DAWNS

Regardless of where women are in their healing journey, moving forward is realizing that there need be no more "hopeless dawns" as long as Christ is in our lives. As women move forward with their lives, there is always hope: hope for a brighter day, hope for greater healing, and hope for a feeling of lasting peace. President Thomas S. Monson has taught about this same hope. In several talks he has given on the Atonement, he has shared an inspiring lesson learned from a painting he discovered in the Tate Gallery in London, England:

> Tucked away in a quiet corner of the third floor was a masterpiece that not only caught my attention, but also captured my heart. The artist, Frank Bramley, had painted a humble cottage facing a wind-swept sea. Kneeling at the side of an older woman was a grief-filled wife who mourned the loss of her seafaring husband. The spent candle at the window ledge told of her fruitless, night-long vigil. The huge gray clouds were all that remained of the tempest-torn night. I sensed her loneliness. I felt her despair. The hauntingly vivid inscription which the artist gave to his work told the tragic story. It read: *A Hopeless Dawn.*[130]

Grief-filled wives who are living with their husband's pornography addiction and are experiencing betrayal trauma or despair have surely faced many hopeless dawns. They have spent days and nights thinking about the tragedy caused by their husbands' pornography use. To them and to all of us, President Dieter F. Uchtdorf has promised the following:

> There may be some among you who feel darkness encroaching upon you. You may feel burdened by worry, fear, or doubt. To you and to all of us, I repeat a wonderful and certain truth: God's light is real. It is available to all! It gives life to all things. (See D&C 88:11–13.) It has the power to soften the sting of the deepest wound. It can be a healing balm for the loneliness and sickness of our souls. In the furrows of despair, it can plant the seeds of a brighter hope. . . . It can illuminate the path before us and lead us through the darkest night into the promise of a new dawn.[131]

This same light will illuminate a new dawn for all who are suffering. There is, and always will be, a brightness of hope made possible through the Atonement of our Savior and Redeemer, Jesus Christ. President Uchtdorf also shared these heartfelt thoughts:

> My heart grieves for the many sorrows some of you face, for the painful loneliness and wearisome fears you may be experiencing. Nevertheless, I bear witness that our living hope is in Christ Jesus! . . . Even after the darkest night, the Savior of the world will lead you to a gradual, sweet, and bright dawn that will assuredly rise within you.[132]

Jesus Christ is the light of the world. It is His love that can penetrate the darkness in all of our lives and turn every hopeless dawn into a joyful morning.

ENDNOTES

INTRODUCTION

1. Boyd K. Packer, "Lehi's Dream and You" (Brigham Young University devotional, January 16, 2007), speeches.byu.edu.
2. All of the names and identifying information of individuals have been changed.
3. John L. Hart and Sarah Jane Weaver, "Defending the Home against Pornography," *Church News*, April 21, 2007.
4. Ibid.
5. "Porn Survey," www.provenmen.org/2014pornsurvey/pornography-use-and -addiction/.
6. Steven Stack, Ira Wasserman, and Roger Kern, "Adult Social Bonds and Use of Internet Pornography," *Social Science Quarterly*, February 11, 2004.
7. Quentin L. Cook, "Can Ye Feel So Now?" *Ensign*, November 2012.
8. John Hilton III and Anthony Sweat, *Why?: Powerful Answers and Practical Reasons for Living LDS Standards* (Salt Lake City: Deseret Book, 2009), 91.
9. Jeffrey R. Holland, quoted in Valerie Johnson, "Elder Holland Speaks at the Utah Coalition against Pornography Conference: 'The Plague of Pornography,'" *Deseret News*, March 12, 2016, m.deseretnews.com/article/865649944/Elder -Holland-speaks-at-the-Utah-Coalition-Against-Pornography-conference-The -Plague-of.html?ref=http%3A%2F%2Fm.facebook.com.
10. Ibid.
11. Dallin H. Oaks, "Recovering from the Trap of Pornography," *Ensign*, October 2015.
12. William M. Struthers, *Wired for Intimacy: How Pornography Hijacks the Male Brain* (Downers Grove, Illinois: InterVarsity Press, 2009), 59.

13. "Definition of Addiction," *American Society of Addiction Medicine*, www .asam.org/for-the-public/definition-of-addiction/.

14. Ibid., emphasis added.

15. "Sexual Addiction Defined," *Relativity*, March 11, 2011, www .sexualrecovery.com/articles/defined.

16. "Sexual Addiction Defined," *Relativity*; Struthers, *Wired for Intimacy*.

17. Struthers, *Wired for Intimacy: How Pornography Hijacks the Male Brain*.

1—BETRAYAL TRAUMA

18. Barbara Steffens and Marsha Means, *Your Sexually Addicted Spouse* (New Horizon Press, 2009).

19. "Betrayal Trauma," *Center for Relational Recovery*, accessed December 21, 2015, www.relationalrecovery.com/trauma-survivors/betrayal-trauma/.

20. Steffens and Means, *Your Sexually Addicted Spouse*.

21. Bridget Kristen Klest, "Trauma, Posttraumatic Symptoms, and Health in Hawaii: Gender, Ethnicity, and Social Context" (doctorate dissertation, Eugene, Oregon, 2010).

22. Robert Weiss, "Understanding Relationship, Sexual, and Intimate Betrayal as Trauma (PTSD)," *PsychCentral*, accessed December 21, 2015, blogs.psychcentral.com/sex/2012/09/understanding-relationship-sexual-and -intimate-betrayal-as-trauma-ptsd/.

23. Jennifer P. Schneider, Robert Weiss, and Charles P. Samenow, "Is It Really Cheating? Understanding the Emotional Reactions and Clinical Treatment of Spouses and Partners Affected by Cybersex Infidelity, Sexual Addiction and Compulsivity," *The Journal of Treatment and Prevention*, 19:123–39 (2012): 134.

24. Steffens and Means, *Your Sexually Addicted Spouse*, 49.

25. Ibid., 30.

26. "Betrayal Trauma," *Center for Relational Recovery*.

27. Weiss, "Understanding Relationship, Sexual, and Intimate Betrayal as Trauma (PTSD)."

28. In the addiction literature, "white knuckle sobriety" means that "the individual is just using pure willpower to stay sober"; "White Knuckle Sobriety," *AlcoholRehab.com*, accessed February 17, 2017, alcoholrehab.com/addiction -recovery/white-knuckle-sobriety/.

29. Emphasis added.

30. Steffens and Means, *Your Sexually Addicted Spouse*, 51.

31. Jeffrey R. Holland, "Lessons from Liberty Jail," *Ensign*, September 2009.

2–DISCOVERY

32. "Our Savior's Love," *Hymns*, no. 113.

33. Steffens and Means, *Your Sexually Addicted Spouse*, 46.

34. Struthers, *Wired for Intimacy: How Pornography Hijacks the Male Brain*, 58.

35. David Schramm, Jennifer Cartel Dochler, Kelly Martinez, "Domestic Violence and Custody Issues," *University of Missouri Extension*.

36. Floyd P. Garrett, "Addiction, Lies and Relationships," *Behavioral Medicine Associates*, 2012, www.bma-wellness.com/papers/Addiction_Lies_Rel.html.

37. Struthers, *Wired for Intimacy: How Pornography Hijacks the Male Brain*, 79.

38. Linda Hatch, "Why Sex Addicts Seem Sociopathic," *PsychCentral*, accessed February 17, 2017, blogs.psychcentral.com/sex-addiction/2012/08/why-sex-addicts-seem-sociopathic/.

39. Rory C. Reid and Dan Gray, *Confronting Your Spouse's Pornography Problem* (Sandy, Utah: Silverleaf Press, 2006), 50.

40. Steffens and Means, *Your Sexually Addicted Spouse*.

41. Mike Fehlauer, "The Invisible Addiction: How One Pastor Defeated a Stronghold through the Power of Jesus Christ," *Krow Tracts*, krowtracts.com/articles/invisible.html.

42. Steffens and Means, *Your Sexually Addicted Spouse*, 61.

43. David Schramm, Jennifer Cartel Dochler, Kelly Martinez, "Domestic Violence and Custody Issues," *University of Missouri Extension*.

3–LOSS OF SELF

44. James E. Faust, "What It Means to Be a Daughter of God," *Ensign*, November 1999.

45. Young Women Theme, www.lds.org/young-women/personal-progress/young-women-theme?lang=eng.

46. Steffens and Means, *Your Sexually Addicted Spouse*, 14.

4—LOSS OF INTIMACY

47. Dave Willis, "9 Steps to Rebuilding Trust in Marriage," *Six Seeds*, August 11, 2016, sixseeds.patheos.com/davewillis/9-steps-rebuilding-trust-marriage/6/.

48. Dallin H. Oaks, "Pornography," *Ensign*, May 2005.

49. M. Russell Ballard, "The Lord Needs You Now!" *Ensign*, September 2015.

50. Struthers, *Wired for Intimacy: How Pornography Hijacks the Male Brain*, 69.

51. Steffens and Means, *Your Sexually Addicted Spouse*, 63.

52. Struthers, *Wired for Intimacy: How Pornography Hijacks the Male Brain*, 59–60.

53. Jeffrey R. Holland, "Place No More for the Enemy of My Soul," *Ensign*, May 2010.

54. Ibid.

55. Wendy Maltz and Larry Maltz, *The Porn Trap: The Essential Guide to Overcoming Problems Caused by Pornography* (Harper, 2008), 182.

56. Struthers, *Wired for Intimacy: How Pornography Hijacks the Male Brain*, 55.

57. Jeffrey R. Holland, "Of Souls, Symbols, and Sacraments" (Brigham Young University devotional, January, 1989), speeches.byu.edu.

58. Douglas Weiss, *Intimacy Anorexia: Healing the Hidden Addiction in Your Marriage* (Discovery Press, 2010), 63.

59. Janice Caudill, "Intimacy Anorexia," *McKinney Counseling and Recovery*, www.drjanicecaudill.com/intimacy-anorexia.html.

60. Douglas Weiss, "Learning How to Recognize and Work with Sexual Anorexia," *Posarc*, accessed December 21, 2015, www.posarc.com/partners/sexual-anorexia.

61. Caudill, "Intimacy Anorexia."

62. Jeffrey R. Holland, "Personal Purity," *Ensign*, November 1998; emphasis added.

5–LOSS OF SPIRITUAL GROUNDING

63. Dieter F. Uchtdorf, "The Why of Priesthood Service," *Ensign*, May 2012.

64. Steffens and Means, *Your Sexually Addicted Spouse*, 117.

65. F. Burton Howard, "Eternal Marriage," *Ensign*, May 2003.

66. Struthers, *Wired for Intimacy: How Pornography Hijacks the Male Brain*, 15.

67. Spencer W. Kimball, *The Miracle of Forgiveness* (Salt Lake City: Bookcraft, 1969), 358.

68. Steffens and Means, *Your Sexually Addicted Spouse*, 122.

69. Jeffrey R. Holland, "The Ministry of Angels," *Ensign*, November 2008.

6—HOPE AND HEALING

70. Ardeth G. Kapp, *Doing What We Came to Do: Living a Life of Love* (Salt Lake City: Deseret Book, 2012), 120.

71. "How Firm a Foundation," *Hymns*, no. 85.

72. Elaine S. Marshall, "Learning the Healer's Art" (Brigham Young University devotional, October 8, 2002), speeches.byu.edu.

73. David Brooks, "What Suffering Does," *New York Times*, April 7, 2014, www.nytimes.com/2014/04/08/opinion/brooks-what-suffering-does.html.

74. "Lord, I Would Follow Thee," *Hymns*, no. 220.

75. Neal A. Maxwell, *All These Things Shall Give Thee Experience* (Salt Lake City: Deseret Book, 1979), 43.

76. Marshall, "Learning the Healer's Art."

77. Richard G. Scott, "To Be Healed," *Ensign*, May 1994.

78. "Kaphar," *Blue Letter Bible*, 2017, www.blueletterbible.org/lang/lexicon/lexicon.cfm?t=kjv&strongs=h3722.

79. See Brad Wilcox, *The Continuous Atonement* (Deseret Book, 2009).

80. Dallin H. Oaks, "He Heals the Heavy Laden," *Ensign*, November 2006.
81. Jeffrey R. Holland, "Where Justice, Love, and Mercy Meet," *Ensign*, May 2015.
82. David A. Bednar, "Bear Up Their Burdens with Ease," *Ensign*, May 2014.
83. David A. Bednar, "Strength beyond Our Own," *New Era*, March 2015.
84. Dieter F. Uchtdorf, "The Gift of Grace," *Ensign*, May 2015.
85. Robert L. Millet, *Grace Works* (Salt Lake City: Deseret Book, 2007), 95.
86. Marshall, "Learning the Healer's Art."
87. Quoted in Spencer W. Kimball, *Faith Precedes the Miracle* (Salt Lake City: Deseret Book, 1972), 98.
88. See David A. Bednar, "In the Strength of the Lord," *Ensign*, November 2004.
89. Guide to the Scriptures, "Grace," scriptures.lds.org.
90. Sheri L. Dew, *Amazed by Grace* (Salt Lake City: Deseret Book, 2015), 21.
91. Bednar, "In the Strength of the Lord."
92. Gene R. Cook, "Receiving Divine Assistance through the Grace of the Lord," *Ensign*, May 1993.
93. Neill F. Marriott, "Yielding Our Hearts to God," *Ensign*, November 2015.
94. Jonathan G. Sandberg, "Healing = Courage + Action + Grace" (Brigham Young University devotional, January 21, 2014), speeches.byu.edu.
95. Jeffrey R. Holland, *Christ and the New Covenant: The Messianic Message of the Book of Mormon* (Salt Lake City: Deseret Book, 1997), 197.

7—MOVING FORWARD

96. Bonnie L. Oscarson, "Defy Gravity: Go Forward with Faith," *New Era*, August 2014.
97. Richard J. Maynes, "The Joy of Living a Christ-Centered Life," *Ensign*, November 2015.
98. Bruce C. Hafen, *Covenant Hearts: Why Marriage Matters and How to Make It Last* (Salt Lake City: Deseret Book, 2005), 125.
99. Brooks, "What Suffering Does."
100. Lorenzo Snow, in Conference Report, April 1899, 2.
101. *Teachings of the Prophet Joseph Smith*, sel. Joseph Fielding Smith (1976), 185.
102. Janis A. Spring, *How Can I Forgive You? The Courage to Forgive, the Freedom Not To* (HarperCollins, 2004), 36.
103. Ibid., 66.
104. Ibid., 15.
105. Richard G. Scott, "Healing the Tragic Scars of Abuse," *Ensign*, May 1992.
106. Virginia H. Pearce, *Extending Forgiveness* (Salt Lake City: Deseret Book, 2013), 49–50.

107. Steve Arteburn, quoted in Cindy Wright, "Rebuilding Trust in Your Marriage," *Marriage Missions*, marriagemissions.com/rebuilding-trust-in-your -marriage/.

108. Donald L. Hilton Jr., *He Restoreth My Soul* (San Antonio, Texas: Forward Press Publishing, 2009), 150–51.

109. Spring, *How Can I Forgive You?*, 176.

110. Ibid., 177.

111. Ibid., 181.

112. Ibid., 182.

113. Ibid.

114. Ibid., 183.

115. Ibid.

116. Boyd K. Packer, "Balm of Gilead," *Ensign*, November 1987.

117. Dieter F. Uchtdorf, "The Merciful Obtain Mercy," *Ensign*, May 2012.

118. Spring, *How Can I Forgive You?*, 89.

119. Spring, *How Can I Forgive You?*, 53.

120. Sterling G. Ellsworth, *Latter-day Plague: Breaking the Chains of Pornography—Causes, Cures, Preventions* (Provo: Maasai Publishing, 2002), 19-20.

121. Spencer W. Kimball, "Jesus: The Perfect Leader," *Ensign*, August, 1979.

122. Hafen, *Covenant Hearts: Why Marriage Matters and How to Make It Last*,

123. Uchtdorf, "The Merciful Obtain Mercy."

124. Dallin H. Oaks, "Divorce," *Ensign*, May 2007.

EPILOGUE

125. Elizabeth Appell, quoted in "Who Wrote 'Risk'? Is the Mystery Solved?," *The Anais Nin Blog*, March 5, 2013, anaisninblog.skybluepress.com/2013/03 /who-wrote-risk-is-the-mystery-solved/.

126. Dieter F. Uchtdorf, "You Are My Hands," *Ensign*, May 2010.

127. Natalie Milne, 1992.

128. See Russell M. Nelson, quoted in *We're with You: Counsel and Encouragement from Your Brethren* (Salt Lake City: Deseret Book, 2016), 116.

129. Neal A. Maxwell, "Why Not Now?," *Ensign*, November 1974.

130. Thomas S. Monson, "Hopeless Dawn—Joyful Morning," *Ensign*, May 1976.

131. Dieter F. Uchtdorf, "The Hope of God's Light," *Ensign*, May 2013.

132. Ibid.

ABOUT THE
AUTHORS

Carmel Parker White has lived in many places in the United States. She grew up in a ranching community in western Montana; received her education in Utah and Kansas; and has taught at universities in Alabama, Kansas, North Carolina, and Utah. She has a doctorate in lifespan human development, which has caused a lifelong interest in the factors that influence the trajectories of people's lives. Using her skills in qualitative interviewing, she was able to draw out women's stories about living with pornography in their marriages. It was a sacred experience to talk with women about their painful journeys, how it altered them, and how they navigated their spiritual experiences with Heavenly Father, with the Atonement, and at church. She is familiar with the impact of pornography in a marriage, as well as spiritual and emotional issues with which women struggle. She has two grown daughters and one granddaughter. She currently lives in Sandy, Utah.

Natalie Black Milne was born and raised in a small southern Utah Mormon community. Although she and her family were devout members of the LDS Church, various types of addiction were prevalent throughout her family tree. She has witnessed firsthand the devastating effects addictions have on individuals and families, as well as the miraculous healing power of the Atonement. Natalie has taken on the challenge

of integrating her background in communication studies with graduate work in family studies at the University of New Mexico, that she not only be up-to-date on the most recent academic research on families in today's world, but also that she might become a voice promoting the sanctity of the family and the essential role the Gospel of Jesus Christ plays in supporting and sustaining the family. She, along with her husband and three sons, lives in Rio Rancho, New Mexico.

Scan to visit

www.loveandbetrayal.net